Picasso
Museum

1

2

3

5

4

7

Picasso
Museum
Paris

The Masterpieces

Marie-Laure Bernadac

Réunion des Musées Nationaux

Prestel

Photographic credits: Réunion des Musées Nationaux, Paris

Translated by Jean Marie Clarke
Edited by Ian Robson

© 1991 by Réunion des Musées Nationaux, Paris (49, rue Etienne Marcel, 75001 Paris) and Prestel-Verlag, Munich

© of Picasso's illustrated works by VG Bild-Kunst, Bonn 1991

© of Brassaï's photographs by Gilberte Brassaï, Paris, 1991

Prestel-Verlag, Mandlstrasse 26, D-8000 Munich 40, Germany
Tel: (89) 38 1709 0; Fax: (89) 38 17 09 35

Distributed in continental Europe by Prestel-Verlag Verlegerdienst München GmbH & Co KG
Gutenbergstrasse 1, D-8031 Gilching, Germany
Tel: (81 05) 21 10; Fax: (81 05) 55 20

Distributed in the USA and Canada by te Neues Publishing Company,
15 East 76th Street, New York, NY 10021, USA
Tel: (212) 288-0265; Fax: (212) 570-2373

Distributed in Japan by YOHAN-Western Publications Distribution Agency,
14-9 Okubo 3-chome, Shinjuku-ku, J-Tokyo 169
Tel: (3) 208 0181; Fax: (3) 209 0288

Distributed in the United Kingdom, Ireland and all remaining countries by Thames & Hudson Limited,
30-40 Bloomsbury Street, London WC1B 3 QP, England
Tel: (71) 636 5488; Fax: (71) 636 4799

Offset lithography by Repro Ludwig GmbH, Zell am See, Austria
Typesetting by Fertigsatz GmbH, Munich
Printing and binding by Passavia Druckerei GmbH, Passau
Printed in Germany

ISBN: 3-7913-1118-2 (English edition)
3-7913-1157-3 (German edition)

Front cover: *The Pipes of Pan*, 1923
Back cover: *Woman with Foliage*, 1934
Half title: *The Jupiter Salon*
Endpapers: Extract from a poem of 24 April 1936
Frontispiece:
1　Picasso and his sister Lola (1884–1958), 1888 (Musée Picasso)

2　Picasso in 1904. Inscribed: "A mes chers amis Suzanne et Henri [Bloch] Picasso 1904" (Musée Picasso)

3　Picasso in Montmartre, c. 1904 (Musée Picasso)

4　Picasso in front of *Construction with Guitar-Player* in progress, in the Boulevard Raspail studio, 1912/13 (Musée Picasso)

5　Picasso with bull's skull, beach of Golfe-Juan, summer 1937 (photo by Dora Maar, Picasso Archives)

6　Picasso in his bedroom at the villa La Galloise, Vallauris, 1954 (photo by Edward Quinn, Picasso Archives)

7　Picasso at La Californie, Cannes, c. 1957/58 (photo by David Douglas Duncan, Picasso Archives)

8　Picasso on the stairs at Rue des Grands-Augustins, 1952 (photo by Denise Colomb, Picasso Archives)

Contents

Introduction

Picasso is doubtless one of the few artists of sufficient stature in our time to warrant the creation of a museum devoted entirely to his life and his work. Considering the sheer bulk of his production, which was due both to his longevity and to his tireless and incessant activity, and the diversity of techniques that he practised—painting, sculpture, engraving, drawing, ceramics, poetry—and also the fact that throughout his life he kept in his possession key works from each period, it seemed only natural to bring these works together in a single museum that would exemplify the many facets of Picasso's art. The museum would of course present Picasso the artist, but also Picasso the man, for in his case life and work were intimately connected, and his friendships with the leading artists, poets, writers, musicians, choreographers and photographers of his time led him to explore many different fields of artistic endeavour: the theatre, ballet, poetry, photography, film. Picasso's genius fully deserves to be characterized as protean. He was a worthy descendant of such great Renaissance figures as Leonardo da Vinci and Michelangelo, who were more than just artists, painters or sculptors, for through their art they acquired a knowledge and prophetic vision of the world that was close to the founding myths of humanity. They were not only the incarnations of their particular historical periods, but geniuses of universal scope.

Picasso seems to have had the idea of a museum in mind for a long time, even if only unconsciously. His whole life long he acquired and carefully preserved paintings by his contemporaries and predecessors, as well as works of primitive art, and was even known to buy back his own canvases on the art market. "What is a painter, after all," he once asked, "if not a collector who wants to assemble a collection by painting himself the pictures he likes by other artists."[1] There was also his interest in the art of the past, his frequent visits to the Louvre, his admiration for paintings in museums, his fetishistic need to keep things. Everything about him points to a predisposition to regard the museum as a special place devoted to aesthetic pleasure and the preservation of memory, and as a facility for learning about art. True, he once declared that "museums are all lies, most of the people involved in art are impostors",[2] but what he was really criticizing were such things as narrow-minded conservativism, academic beauty, official art, the museum as mausoleum.

Picasso died intestate, leaving behind a colossal estate that included thousands of works of art. The effective basis for the creation of the museum was provided by the French law of *dation*, which permits heirs to donate works of art in lieu of paying estate duty. Picasso's legal heirs were Maya, his daughter with Marie-Thérèse Walter, Claude and Paloma, his children with Françoise Gilot, Marina and Bernard, the children of his son Paulo, and his wife, Jacqueline Picasso. They generously agreed to waive their right of designation and allow the state to have first choice of the works to be presented. Dominique Bozo, Curator of the Réunion des Musées Nationaux, had the daunting and delicate task of selecting from among these thousands of works those that might constitute a suitable collection for a museum. He was assisted and guided therein by friends and historians who had known Picasso: Jean Leymarie, Roland Penrose, Pierre Daix. A variety of criteria had to be satisfied: to give both a technical and a chronological overview, to reveal aspects long unknown to the public (because jealously kept secret by Picasso), to highlight preparatory works and series, and of course to assemble a core of "masterpieces". The first *dation* of 1979 comprised 203 paintings, 158 sculptures, 28 *tableaux-reliefs*, 16 *papiers collés*, 88 ceramic pieces, over 3,000 prints and drawings, 34 sketchbooks, many illustrated books and manuscripts, works by other artists, and part of Picasso's collection of Primitive Art. The master's personal

For the notes see p. 206.

◁ Picasso Museum, façade on the garden side

collection of paintings by Cézanne, Matisse, Braque, Rousseau and Derain, which had been donated to the Louvre in 1973,[3] was subsequently incorporated in the Picasso Museum, where it serves to evoke the past and present aesthetic context of his life's work. Since the museum's opening, its collections have been further enriched by acquisitions and gifts, the most recent and spectacular of which were the *Three Figures under a Tree* of 1907/08, a gift from Mr. McCarthy Cooper, and *Celestina* (1904), a highly significant painting from the artist's Blue Period.

The next thing to be done was to find a place to house the collection, a building worthy of and in harmony with Picasso's work. Judging from the houses where he lived and worked—the Château de Boisgeloup, the Hôtel des Grands-Augustins, the Villa La Californie in Cannes, the Château de Vauvenargues, the *mas* Notre-Dame de Vie at Mougins—we can deduce that he had a particular fondness for antique and monumental dwelling-places. Thus, the Hôtel Salé, a seventeenth-century mansion situated in the historic heart of Paris, where the artist had lived for many years, seemed a most fitting home for his museum.

Wealth, no matter how great, always seems to attract more wealth. Eleven years after the first *dation*, a second batch of works, smaller, but every bit as exciting and poignant, came to augment the Picasso Museum. Following the death of Jacqueline Picasso, the painter's second wife, on 15 October 1986, her daughter, Catherine Hutin-Blay, ceded a number of works of art toward the payment of death duties. The final selection represented a considerable enrichment of the national heritage: 47 paintings, 2 sculptures, 40 drawings, 24 sketchbooks, 19 ceramic pieces, and 245 engravings and lithographs. A collage by Braque, *Tivoli Cinema* (1913), one of his masterpieces from the Cubist period, came with the Picasso works. A large portion of this *dation* went to the Picasso Museum to fill gaps and complete various series, while other important works were installed on permanent loan in other French museums, including the Musée Picasso in Antibes and the Musée National d'Art Moderne at the Centre Georges Pompidou.

If Picasso stands out as the best-known artist of the twentieth century, his work may nevertheless be the least well known, having so to speak been eclipsed by his worldwide fame and the near-mythic legends of money and love-affairs that surround it. Thus, the opening of the Picasso Museum to the public in September 1986 came as nothing less than a major cultural revelation. Art-lovers, both neophytes and *aficionados*, now have a chance to judge the works on their own terms, to cut through the prejudices that had obscured a clear vision of them, to learn to see, understand and love them.

For a long time, and for not a few even today, Picasso's name was synonymous with modern art and as such tended to have a pejorative connotation: in front of a work that was particularly difficult to read, the perplexed viewer would declare: "That could be a Picasso." The group of works in this museum in fact presents several artists in one: there is Picasso the Cubist, Picasso the Surrealist, Picasso the revolutionary, Picasso the classic, a Picasso both tragic and comical. We can see the various paths explored by this elusive figure, this veritable Janus inspired alternately by Apollo and Dionysus. The rooms are disposed like an Ariadne's thread to lead visitors through the labyrinthine mystery of creation, and, where Picasso's work is concerned, there are many ways in and out, many prefigurations and reemergences. Each generation has had its own vision of Picasso. For a long time there was a preference for his Cubist phase, the rigour of his formal inventions, which were so decisive for the evolution of twentieth-century art. Then came the politically involved Picasso of *Guernica*, later a member of the Communist party and a media figure. There was also the misunderstood Picasso, the Picasso of the last years, recently reassessed and reinstated in his true role as a key figure in contemporary painting. The major exhibitions devoted to the "realisms" of the twenties highlighted Picasso's classical side. Today, thanks to the specific character of the museum's collections, the visitor can rediscover a "Picasso furioso"[4] on the fringes of the Surrealist movement, whose poetic, erotic and passionate forms exploded on the scene with the greatest creative charge of their time.

Picasso is at the focus of every artistic invention of the twentieth century, and he left his mark on nearly every realm of creative activity. His work is very much alive, because it can always be rediscovered, teaching us not only about art, but also about enthusiasm and humanity.

This book presents a selection of approximately one hundred works that are considered to be among the museum's masterpieces: works of undeniable historical importance, but also less well-known works that Picasso jealously kept for himself, either for personal and sentimental reasons, or because they were significant milestones or turning-points in his career. These works were chosen from among the periods best represented in the museum's collection: the Cubist constructions, the Neoclassical Period, the Boisgeloup Period, and the last years. We have alternated paintings with sculptures in broadly chronological order so as to bring out the continuous dialogue between these two modes of expression during the artist's career. Each entry gives a formal description, establishes correspondences with related works in the museum, presents preparatory drawings and recognized sources, and places the work within the context of the artist's life and stylistic development. The ultimate purpose of the book is to provide the reader with a set of keys to unlock the very special world of Picasso.

Finally, we would like to thank Marie Cerciello for editing the commentaries 1, 3, 4, 7, 10, 11, 12, 16, 19, 24, 27, 40, 59, 72, 75, 76, 77, 83, 86, 90, 98 and 102; Hélène Seckel, chief curator of the Picasso Museum for editing nos. 35, 80, 81, 87; and Brigitte Léal for no. 92.

The Hôtel Salé

The decision to install such modern, and often provocative, works in a seventeenth-century mansion was not uncontroversial. Some people were offended by what they considered to be a slight to their historical heritage, while others felt that Picasso deserved a more innovative setting. Yet, in the light of the result, it may be said that there has rarely been such a successful harmonization of the old and the new, of the past and the present. Interesting relationships are created, as between the classical and monumental *Three Women at the Fountain* (1921) or the *Bust of Marie-Thérèse* (1932) and the ornamental sculptures of the grand staircase. The houses in which Picasso lived also show that he had a fondness for old dwellings.

The establishment of a Picasso museum in Paris, where the artist lived for many years, is very appropriate. The Hôtel Salé, located at no. 5, rue de Thorigny, is—along with the Hôtel Rohan-Soubise, which houses the National Archives—one of the largest mansions in the historic Marais du Temple quarter. In 1656 two lots of land belonging to the nuns of Saint-Gervais were purchased by Aubert de Fontenay, collector of the salt tax, hence the nickname *salé* that the Parisians gave to the *hôtel* he had built in 1659.

"The house was built by the architect Jean Boullier (also known as Jean de Bourges), and is composed of a main building of emphatic design with a garden on one side and a courtyard on the other. The oval shape of the courtyard, which permitted carriages to manoeuvre more easily, was an innovation at the time. To the right, the courtyard is flanked by the low-lying outbuildings, which are topped by a terrace with a balustrade joined to the main building by a console decorated with a sphinx. This wing separates the main courtyard from a smaller courtyard adjacent to the stables. On the left, the semicircle is completed by a wall topped by a similar balustrade joined to the house by a sphinx.

"The main building is composed of a ground floor, a first storey or *piano nobile*, and a second, attic storey, crowned by a vast mansard roof. A large curvilinear pediment spans the three main bays of the façade; it is decorated with a coat-of-arms featuring a helmet and scrolls held by hounds and female figures in high relief connected by festoons to some very healthy-looking putti. The façade on the garden side is not centred on the same axis as the one overlooking the courtyard; it is flanked by two pavilions and occupies the entire width of the building. The pediment on the second storey is triangular and decorated with sculpted hounds and scrollwork.

"From the main entrance one has a splendid view of the stucco decoration of the staircase, composed of winged figures holding garlands of fruits that frame medallions containing busts. On the cornice, in the midst of garlands, the intertwined initials of Aubert and his wife, *née* Chastelain, are to be seen. The staircase leads to the Salon de Jupiter, which is also splendidly decorated with putti, garlands, and two medallions with reclining gods. This sculpted decoration is the work of Martin Desjardins, who was born in Breda in 1640 and came to France as a young man. Immediately after executing the sculptures of the Hôtel Salé, he worked on the decoration of the Hôtel Beauvais, which we know was finished in 1660."[1]

The building was put to various uses over the years. In 1671 it was rented to the Venetian Embassy. In 1768 it was renamed Hôtel de Juigné, because the then owner, Philibert Thiroux de Chammeville, gave the house in dowry to his daughter when she wed the Marquis de Juigné. In 1793 it became the Dépôt National Littéraire, a library of books seized in monasteries during the Revolution, and in 1818 an educational establishment for boys. Between 1829 and 1884 it housed the École Centrale des Arts et Manufactures. In 1887 it was leased by the bronzesmith Vian, who displayed his production in its

View of the façade on the courtyard side

façades: first those of the main building, then those of the outbuildings, and finally the outer walls. During this period the chapel, the caretaker's lodge, and the grand staircase were also restored. Roland Simounet won the competition for the conversion of the interior to museum use, and work was commenced on the realization of his plans in May 1983. Restoration of the woodwork, the walls of the grand staircase, and the pavement of the courtyard (under the direction of M. Fonquernie, Head

The Man with the Sheep

salons. From 1945 to 1960 it was the home of the École des Métiers d'Art. In 1962 the City of Paris acquired the now deserted mansion, which was declared a historic monument in 1968 and subsequently leased to the state for the establishment of the Musée Picasso.

When it became the property of the City of Paris, the Hôtel Salé was in a very dilapidated state. It was not yet classed as a listed building, and thus only summary repairs were effected at the time. It was only after the Picasso museum project was announced in 1974 that a true restoration campaign could be conducted under the direction of M. Vitry, then Head Architect of Historic Monuments. During 1974 and 1975 priority work to protect the building from water damage (roofing) and to repair the masonry of the cornices was undertaken. The second phase, which was commenced in 1976 and completed in 1980, concerned the masonry of the

The Salon de Jupiter seen from the grand staircase, with Diego Giacometti's lantern ▷

The Salon de Jupiter

The Salon de Jupiter

Architect of Historic Monuments) was undertaken only after the first museum installations had been effected. The design of the museum's furnishings—chairs, tables, benches, chandeliers on the first floor and lantern—was entrusted to the sculptor Diego Giacometti, whose style was eminently suited to the monumentality of the house and the spirit of Picasso's art.

The museum respects the prestigious elements of this remarkable historical monument: the foyer, the grand staircase, and the Salon de Jupiter with its superb stonework decoration. The proportions of the interior spaces, destroyed by later additions—walls and intermediate floors that hid the fine old woodwork—have been restored to their original grandeur. The old ceilings of the suite of rooms on the first floor have been restored. There are parquet floors on the upper storey, and flagstones on the ground-floor and basement levels. The main building provides accommodation for the permanent collection in the basement and on the ground and first floors (1,372 m^2) and for special exhibitions on the second floor (278 m^2). The semi-public and private areas—the department of drawings, the library, and the curatorial offices—are located on the upper levels. Public spaces in the outbuildings include a small projection-room in the basement and a reception area, ticket-booth, cafeteria and service facilities on the ground floor. The second courtyard was covered with a skylight and is used for the display of sculptures.

The display of the works is basically chronological with a few thematic and technical exceptions (the "Bathers", ceramics, sculpture), and adapted to the variations of the architectural features.

The grand staircase leads visitors to the first floor, where the tour begins. The first rooms on the front court side retain their former aspect; they are relatively small and well suited to the works of the Blue and Rose periods presented there. The visit continues with the suite of rooms in which Cubist and Classical works are displayed. From the first floor, ramps lead to the special exhibition rooms on the second floor. The "Bathers" and works from the Boisgeloup Period are shown on the garden level, and also in the sculpture-garden located in the former service-yard. The basement is occupied by

The sculpture garden

The staircase to the second floor

Room 16 with the plaster original of *The Goat* ▷

The ceramics room

Room 14, with *Fernande*

works from the grim war years. Visitors take a staircase from there back to the garden level, where they can see works from the last period. A transition room leads outside to the garden, where a number of monumental sculptures are on display. There seems to be such harmony between the works and the space they occupy that one would think the house had been destined for this purpose from the very beginning. Consider, for example, the high, light-filled rooms with works from Boisgeloup, the descent into the basement and the dramatic period of the war years, and the return to the light for the painter's glorious Mediterranean apotheosis. We hope that our visitors will enjoy their encounter with this historic building and the timeless works of art it contains.

The Blue Period

1 The Death of Casagemas
La mort de Casagemas

When Picasso returned to Paris from Spain in the summer of 1901, the Catalan painter Pere Man-yach and the art critic Gustave Coquiot organized an exhibition of his work at Ambroise Vollard's gallery. The artist moved into the Boulevard de Clichy studio previously occupied by his friend Casagemas, who had committed suicide a few months before over an unhappy love affair.

The tragedy gradually began to obsess Picasso. To exorcise it, he executed a series of posthumous portraits comprising seven canvases and a number of drawings.[1] First he portrayed his friend lying in state, then he celebrated a burial ceremony inspired by El Greco[2]—whose manneristically elongated figures were to become a constant feature of the Blue Period—and finally he resurrected him in a painting titled Life (La Vie, 1903, The Cleveland Museum of Art).

Here we see only the face of the suicide emerging from a shroud; it is shown close up, in profile, with the wound in the temple caused by the fatal bullet. To counter this strong diagonal form, Picasso added a large candle, which radiates its light throughout the painting. This traditional symbol of the brevity of life often appears in the still-lifes he painted during the Second World War. The candle casts yellow streaks of light on the shroud and outlines the profile; its flickering contrasts with the immobility and timeless character of the face. The influence of Van Gogh is obvious in the brushwork and the red, yellow, blue and green impasto.

"It was because I had Casagemas on my mind that I began to paint in blue", he later revealed to Pierre Daix. His friend's death provoked a transformation in his painting: after the pre-Fauvist works exhibited at Vollard's in June, Picasso progressively reduced his palette to a blue monochrome, which was to characterize his paintings until 1904.

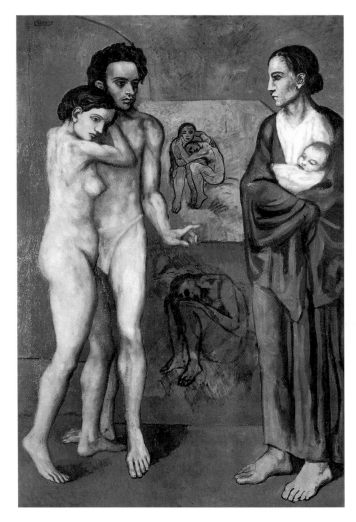

Life, 1903, The Cleveland Museum of Art

The Burial of Casagemas, 1901, Musée d'Art Moderne, Paris

1 *The Death of Casagemas*, summer 1901, Paris. Oil on wood, 27 x 35 cm

The Suicide Victim, 1901, private collection

2 Self-Portrait

Autoportrait

Like Rembrandt and Van Gogh, his illustrious predecessors in the genre, Picasso seems to have had
a predilection for the self-portrait, where the exter-
nal image of the man becomes infused with the
subjective projection of the artist; throughout his
long career he painted various likenesses of himself
that reveal his progress in life and art. The present
work, painted during his second stay in Paris in the
winter of 1901, was the end of a series and marked
the beginning of the Blue Period. He returned to
Barcelona in January 1902.

Picasso was only twenty years old at the time,
but he appears considerably older in this portrait.
His face is drawn and gaunt from the hardships of
the Parisian winter. The livid pallor of the face, relieved only by the orange tint of the lips, the
scraggy beard, and the high-collared greatcoat
that enshrouds the body, all heighten the feeling of
sadness and solitude that emanates from the canvas. The use of cool tones, especially the deep purple of the coat, and the light, almost "anaemic"
brushwork overall—except in the face—are completely in keeping with the stark, ascetic image. The
fluid contour of the greatcoat, which is treated in
broad, vertical areas separated by a black line,
recalls the influence of Toulouse-Lautrec and Gauguin. The psychological intensity expressed in the
artist's sombre and almost hallucinatory gaze is reminiscent of self-portraits by Van Gogh. The shape
of the coat and the layout of the composition were
later repeated almost identically in the *Celestina*
portrait (pl. 3).

In this uncompromising vision of himself, Picasso
makes no secret of the trials and tribulations that
beset the young artist, but he does not fall prey to
sentimentality. The Spaniard still has his pride.

The Blue Period is characterized by an extreme
melancholy, and this is the feature that struck contemporary critics the most: "It is an extraordinary
thing, the sterile sadness that pervades the work of
this very young man. . . . This frighteningly preco-
cious child may well be destined to consecrate with
his masterpieces the negative sense of life, that
curse from which he suffers more than all others."[3]

Self-Portrait, 1897,
private collection

Self-Portrait, "Yo Picasso", 1901, private collection

2 *Self-Portrait*, late 1901, Paris. Oil on canvas, 81 x 60 cm ▷

Picasso's friend and factotum Sabartès tells us: "He believes that sadness is conducive to meditation and that pain is the foundation of life."[4] Charles Morice attributes this "fondness for the gestures and accents of grief" to the atavistic influence of his Andalusian origins.

A satisfactory explanation of the Blue Period has yet to be given. Actually, there are two things to consider: on the one hand, the monochromatic palette, and on the other, the colour blue. There is no lack of psychological and symbolic interpretations of this colour, which is naturally associated with night. Jung speaks of "the blue of night, of moonlight, and of water, the blue of Tuat, god of the Egyptian hell".[5] The use of a monochromatic palette implies certain pictorial consequences, such as simplification, stylization and unification. It is also, as Pierre Daix has noted, the first transgression of visible appearances, an assertion of the painter's own subjectivity; he shows everything in blue, as if he were looking at the world through a filter. Alberto Moravia seems to have understood exactly what was at stake in this period, for he says that "blue means neither misery, nor hunger . . . . It underlines Picasso's wilful intention to assert his own very specific vitality, without judgment or moral choice, by means of a totalitarian and demiurgic colour."[6]

models. Her face is treated with great realism: grey hair swept back, hairy chin and tense jaw, the ear adorned with a modest earring. The slight rose tint of the cheeks announces the end of the Blue Period.

Prostitution is a subject that often recurs in the artist's work. Picasso treated the theme of Celestina again in 1968 in a series of 66 etchings and aquatints to illustrate a deluxe edition of Rojas's classic.

Unusual about this picture is that it does not display the pathos so characteristic of the other figures of the Blue Period. There is no self-pity. Celestina emerges from an indefinite background, darting a one-eyed glance obliquely over the viewer's shoulder. This questioning eye looking out upon the world is omnipresent. Gérard Régnier describes the picture in the following terms: "The figure of Celestina—both procuress and witch casting spells with her evil eye, charged with the malefic powers that folktales and legends attribute to the one-eyed—haunted Picasso throughout his life and work. This woman-become-eye gazing upon the carnal doings of mankind presents the painter, that guardian and destroyer of appearances, with the image of his own destiny."

3 Celestina
La Célestine

Picasso, who was very fond of Spanish literature, was familiar with the tragicomedy of Calixto and Melibea written by Fernando de Rojas in 1499, in which the heroine, a go-between named Celestina, resorts to money to overcome Melibea's resistance to Calixto's advances. It was in Barcelona that Picasso discovered Carlota Valdivia, the model for his portrayal of the legendary procuress.

The pencil and pastel sketches show a woman of uncommon ugliness, but in the final painting she seems more human, despite the fact that she has only one healthy eye. Wrapped in a dark cape that sets off her features, the procuress wears a hood like the diseased prostitutes of the prison-hospital Saint-Lazare in Paris, where Picasso also found

Study for Celestina, 1904, private collection

3 *Celestina*, March 1904, Barcelona. Oil on canvas, 70 × 56 cm

The Rose Period

4 The Fool
Le fou

In 1904, Picasso definitively established himself in
Paris, where he now had a wide circle of friends:
Marie Laurencin, Derain, Braque, Vlaminck, Modi-
gliani, Max Jacob, etc. He was fascinated by the
world of the big top and often went to the Médrano
Circus with them. "We were always at the Médrano", Fernande Olivier, his companion, recalls,
"we would go there three or four times a week."
She also tells us that he "liked to linger at the bar,
amid the warm and somewhat heady smells from
the stables. He would stay there with Braque, talking
all evening with the clowns. He liked their ungainly
manner, their accents, their repartee."[1]

The fool or jester first appears in Picasso's work
in 1905. Harlequin is the most characteristic figure
of the Rose Period, and he is never represented as
sophisticated or courteous, or playing the buffoon
on front stage, but rather as a tender and sensitive
figure in the intimate surroundings of his family and
the circus animals. The artist must have felt a certain kinship with this solitary and wandering figure
who lived on the fringes of society like him.

Picasso began to work on the sculpture *The Fool*
late one evening after returning from the Médrano
with Max Jacob, his neighbour at the Bateau-
Lavoir. At first he wanted to do his friend's portrait,
but when he resumed work on it the next day, the
head acquired a new personality; only the lower
part of the face reproduces the poet's features. The
analogy between the artist and the fool, both out-
siders, is now clearly expressed.

The bust, cast in bronze by Ambroise Vollard,
has a rugged solidity enhanced by the play of light
on the features. The strong contrasts made by the
ridges and hollows that reflect or absorb the light
are accentuated by the deep-set eyes and the jagged forms of the cap. This stark relationship between light and shadow is what creates the forms,
rather than any detailed realism in the rendition of
the face. The bust should be viewed in three-quar-
ter profile, an angle the artist often used in his subsequent painted and sketched portraits. Such a
vantage-point reveals the figure's personality, its
peculiar sensitivity, enigmatic smile and dreamy
gaze, which seems to be pondering on the human
condition.

Mountebank Kneeling before a Crowned Mountebank,
1905, Musée Picasso, Paris

The Two Brothers, 1905, Kunstmuseum, Basle

The Adolescents, 1905, National Gallery of Art, Washington

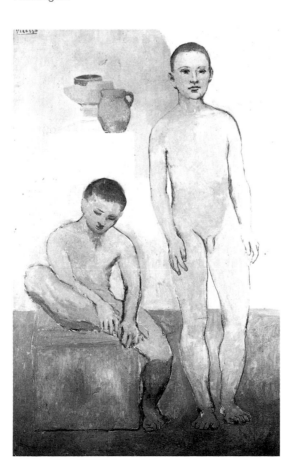

5   The Two Brothers
Les deux frères

Picasso spent most of the summer of 1906 with his companion Fernande Olivier in Gósol, a small village in upper Catalonia. This sojourn marked a new phase in his work, although a sharp change had already been announced in 1905 with the "Mountebanks" series. He abandoned the sentimental and literary aesthetic of the Blue Period, the emaciated faces, the visions of solitude and sadness, in favour of a more radiant world, full of beauty, harmony and serenity. The theme of the two boys, their delicately drawn, pensive features expressing brotherly tenderness, and the presence of the drum are leftovers from the circus world. But the nudity, the volumetric treatment of the bodies, the stable frontal stance, and the warm ochre, grey and pink tones herald Picasso's new "classicizing" style. This gouache from the beginning of his stay in Gósol was a study for the large painting in Basle of the same subject, for which a number of preparatory sketches have been preserved.[2] In the Basle picture the accessories have been left out, and the nude figure advances slightly in profile against an entirely monochrome ground. In the present work, Picasso has combined the representation of a nude youth with still-life elements to create a pictorial rhythm; but the terracotta bowl and jug with flowers are also Mediterranean accessories, allusions to his simple and rustic life with Fernande at Gósol.

Picasso emphasizes the sculptural treatment of the bodies: torso and legs are simplified into rounded volumes, an effect of relief being created by the interplay of lighter and warmer fleshy tones. The full forms of the bodies stand out against a plain background, and the handling of the torso and legs is reminiscent of the stylization of archaic sculpture. The somewhat indistinct treatment of the upper torso reappears in *The Two Women* of 1906.[3]

4 *The Fool*, 1905, Paris. Bronze, 41.5 x 37 x 22.8 cm

5 *The Two Brothers*, summer 1906, Gósol. Gouache on cardboard, 80 x 59 cm ▷

6 Self-Portrait
Autoportrait

This self-portrait from the last phase of the Gósol period belongs to a series that includes the *Self-Portrait with a Palette* (Philadelphia Museum of Art) and many drawings (with several sketches sometimes superimposed on the same sheet) in which Picasso studied his own face as if it were a mask.

The torso is built like an architecture: square, bordered by three dark lines formed by the edges of the arms and the collarbone, whose centre coincides with the axis of the pectorals and the chest. The neck is handled like a plain cylinder, which means that this self-portrait might have been painted after the one in Philadelphia, for the latter still respects the curved contour of the neck. The oval-shaped head seems to rest on a thickset, broad and robust chest that owes as much to the influence of Cézanne's *Large Bather* (1885/87, The Museum of Modern Art, New York) as to the painter's own anatomy. The face presents the characteristic features of the Gósol period and of Iberian statuary: arched eyebrows, triangular nose and outlined eyelids. However, here the eyes do not reveal a void, but the artist's dark and piercing gaze. The asymmetrical handling of the forehead not only mysteriously broadens the gaze, but also anticipates to a certain extent the combined frontal and profile views in the later portraits.

After the Rose Period, Picasso returned in this work to the greyish and muted coloration that was to become characteristic of Cubism. The paint is dense, thickly spread and modulated, the brushwork seeming to sculpt and mould the forms. An overall impression of strength, robustness and serenity is created. Alfred Barr remarks that, in just a few months, "the artist moved from a near Praxitelean style toward an archaic austerity",[4] as if he had understood the reason for the stiffness and awkwardness of the antique *kouroi*. We get the impression that the body will not long be able to resist the tension that swells its forms, the vital force that tightens the muscles beneath the skin.

The most interesting thing about this painting, apart from the pictorial and stylistic innovations, is the fixedness and sharpness of the gaze. "The eye,

Studies for a Self-Portrait, 1906, Musée Picasso, Paris

simple almond or dark abyss, the only window through which distress and anguish show themselves."[5] Like a deep well plunging into the depths behind the painting, the eye is an essential feature of Picasso's work. The transformation of perception, the primacy of the visible, a window either open or closed, a questioning of the spectator, his view of the world or of himself, all this is contained in the dark pupil of Picasso's eye.

Self-Portrait with Palette, 1906, Museum of Art, Philadelphia

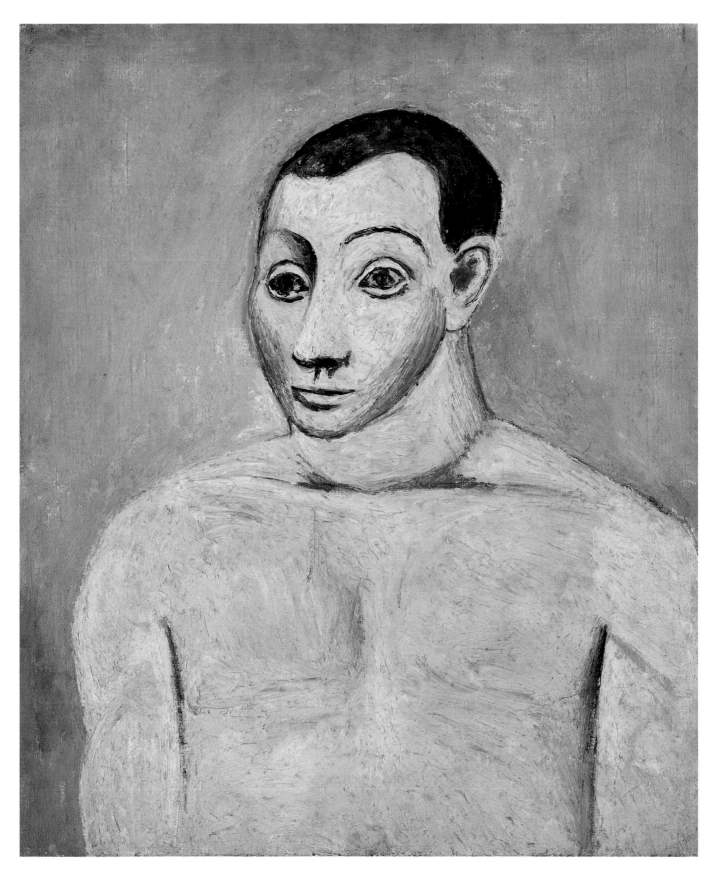

6 *Self-Portrait*, autumn 1906, Paris. Oil on canvas, 65 x 54 cm

The Demoiselles Period

7 Seated Nude
Nu assis

This statuesque figure with the massive, detailed chest, the sex hidden from view by a leg resting on the knee, arms stretched out and holding the leg, was a study for *Les demoiselles d'Avignon* (1907, New York, Museum of Modern Art, New York). The body has a masculine appearance, but the hair framing the face would suggest that it is a woman. This sexual ambiguity characterizes other figures in the *Demoiselles* as well. There is something paradoxical about the way the nude is seated, its apparent stability contradicted by the unbalanced pose. A mysterious, timeless quality is suggested by the woman's face, nodding forward with eyes closed as if she were sleeping.

The blue curtain creates depth without the use of traditional perspectival devices. The expressionless, mask-like face displays the influence of Iberian statuary[1] that first appeared in the heads of Fernande from Gósol (*Reclining Nude*, 1906, The Cleveland Museum of Art) and culminated in the

Bust of a Woman with Joined Hands (Study for *Les Demoiselles d'Avignon*), 1907, Musée Picasso, Paris

Portrait of Gertrude Stein (1906, The Metropolitan Museum of Art, New York). The head of the *Seated Nude* is stylized, the face reduced to an oval: the ear stands out larger than life, the nose extends the line of the eyebrows, the almond-shaped eyes are strongly outlined. The torso seems to be the schematization of an academic bust, here and there scored with black lines.

Of the various studies for the *Demoiselles*, this is the figure that underwent the greatest degree of transformation. In the first studies, it had the same seated position. "Then she opens her legs, uncovers the triangle of her sex, which the cloth held in the left hand no longer conceals, and raises her right arm above her head in an academic pose."[2] The seat has disappeared, and the figure becomes a reclining nude represented vertically.

Bust of a Woman (Study for *Les Demoiselles d'Avignon*), 1907, Musée Picasso, Paris

7 *Seated Nude*, winter 1906/07, Paris. Oil on canvas, 121 × 93.5 cm ▷

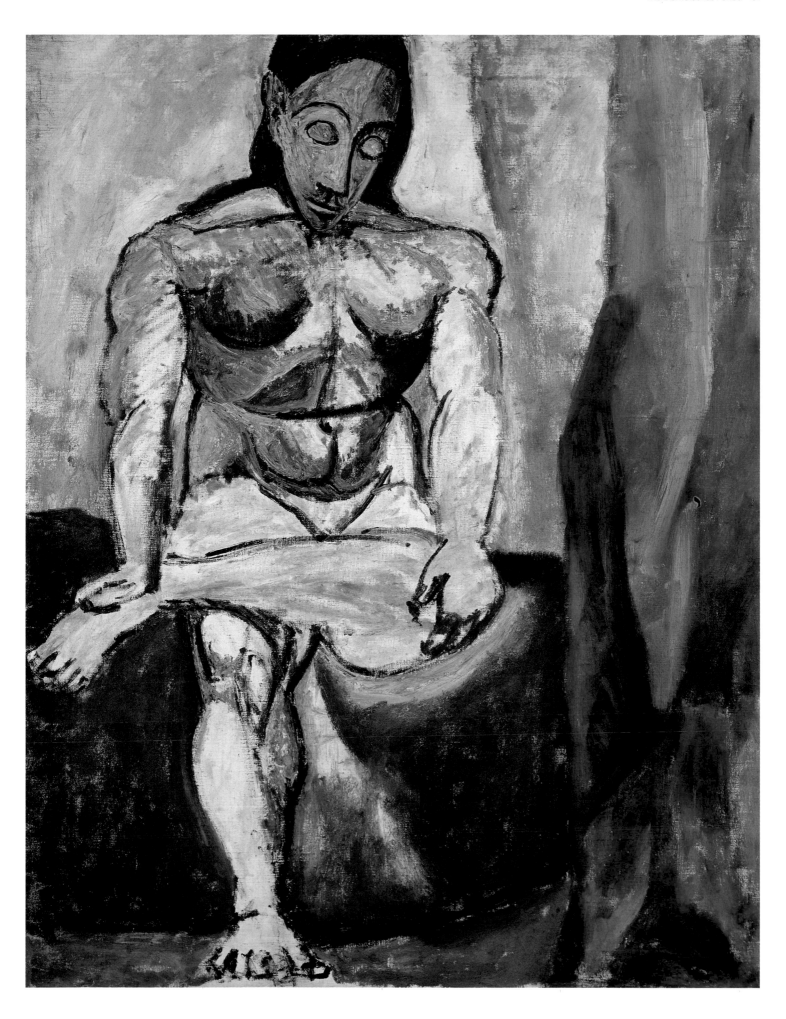

8 Mother and Child

Mère et enfant

Everything about this picture makes it an exceptional work in Picasso's painting of this period: the violently contrasting colours—blue, red, green—the extreme stylization of the faces, the massive bodies like tailor's dummies, the coarse features of the child; it is indeed a most unusual representation of the theme of motherhood. The use of hatching on the faces and parts of the background allows us to date it right after *Les demoiselles d'Avignon*, which it follows like an afterthought, and shortly before the *Nude with Drapery* of the same year (Hermitage Museum, St. Petersburg). The hatching here is vigorously coloured and no longer serves simply to indicate shading or suggest relief, as it does in the *Bust of a Woman (or Sailor)*. The purpose of the strokes is to create a pictorial rhythm that integrates figure and background. These linear patterns should not be confused with the ritual scars of African art, which are always symmetrical; in Picasso's painting they emphasize the dissymmetry. The disproportionate eyes and noses recall the conventions of Iberian sculpture, but pushed to the extreme. The woman's face derives directly from some of the female studies for the *Demoiselles*, especially the form of her chignon and of her nose and eyes. The face of the child, with its huge eyes, tiny oval mouth, linear patterns, and expressive force, is more reminiscent of African masks. This last figure is rather curious, closer to a marionette or an old man than to a child. The peculiar form of the head, with its expanse of red paint instead of hair, creates the impression of an empty skull and accentuates the feeling of strangeness.

There is something of Matisse in the formal simplification, the flat colours, the geometricized background and the primitive appearance of the whole. Picasso particularly admired the raw simplicity of Matisse's *Portrait of Marguerite* (Musée Picasso, Paris), which he already owned in 1907.

The theme of motherhood occurs in Picasso's work at particular times: during the Blue and Rose periods, and in the twenties, after the birth of his son Paulo. It is surprising to find it as the subject of a painting in 1907, among iconographical preoccupations of an entirely different order. Is this figure an allusion to the child "adopted" by Fernande, or a transposition of the student or the sailor from the study for the *Demoiselles*? In the latter case, it might again be the image of Picasso, or of Max Jacob, in the company of one of those flighty "young ladies"—Fernande, Marie Laurencin, or even Max Jacob's grandmother—as Picasso provocatively liked to identify them.

Bust of a Woman or Sailor (Study for *Les Demoiselles d'Avignon*), 1907, Musée Picasso, Paris

8 *Mother and Child*, summer 1907, Paris. Oil on canvas, 81 x 60 cm ▷

9 Figure

Figure

This roughly carved figure with touches of paint is contemporary with *Les demoiselles d'Avignon*. Its spirit and its forms reveal the primitivistic influence under which Picasso was working at the time: that of Gauguin first of all, then of African and Oceanic art. Picasso was well acquainted with Gauguin's wood sculptures thanks to the major retrospective that had been held at the Salon d'Automne in 1906, and through his compatriot and neighbour at the Bateau-Lavoir, the sculptor Paco Durio. What appealed to Picasso in Gauguin's work was not so much its exoticism as the return to more primitive and savage forms of expression. Picasso also had in his collection a *tiki* from the Marquesas Islands and two statues from New Caledonia that present a similar geometric simplification of volumes: the body is inscribed in a rectangle, which gives the figure a stocky, massive appearance, the parts of the body being stacked vertically. Preparatory sketches show that the first version of this female idol was draped. The Picasso Museum possesses a drawing of the sculpture with brightly coloured hatchings analogous to the rough carving of the wood.

This *Figure* is the most monumental of the eight wood sculptures that Picasso made at this time. The body is shown frontally, crudely modelled, barely emerging from the block of wood. Some areas, like

Figure, 1907, Musée Picasso, Paris

the face and the right arm, have even been left uncarved. The lines painted on the face and belly enhance the definition of the forms. The most exceptional feature of the work, however, is the brutal way in which the wood has been carved, as if it had been set upon with a hatchet. This violent treatment is apparent in the deep grooves and sharp edges of the forms around the breasts. The material retains all of its raw vitality; the grain of the wood and the marks of the tools remain visible. The coarse surfaces and crisp texture give this female idol an "untouchable" aspect.

The strength, freedom and solidity of the work is close to the vision of woman expressed in the *Demoiselles*. This impression is accentuated by the simian mask of the face, the tension between the form and the material expressed in the squatness of the figure, and the *non-finito*, a feature that was peculiar to Picasso, but not to primitive art.

Standing Nude in Profile, 1908, Musée Picasso, Paris

9 *Figure*, 1907, Paris.
Oak with painted highlights,
80.5 x 24 x 20.8 cm

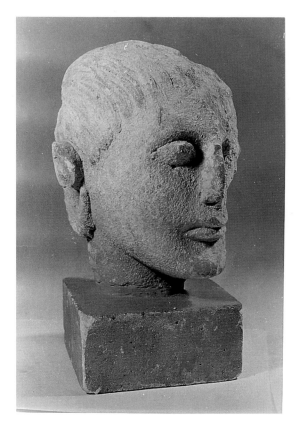

Male Head, Iberian sculpture, 5th-3rd cent. B.C., Musée des Antiquités Nationales, Saint-Germain-en-Laye

Male Head, 1907, Musée Picasso, Paris

10   The Nude with Raised Arms

Le nu aux bras levés

During 1908, Picasso pursued the "African" stylization that he had already experimented with in *Les demoiselles d'Avignon.*

As in many tribal masks, this nude with raised arms is half-human, half-animal. The face is dominated by a prominent nose that looks more like a snout, the forehead curves broadly, and the form of the leg is closer to that of a quadruped than that of a human being. The woman is devoid of personality or expressivity, she has been reduced to a more primitive existence through formal simplification. She stretches herself, raising her arms behind her head, a pose that makes her breasts and belly project forward. She seems animated by slow, heavy motion. The bewitching eroticism of the figure is heightened by the low viewpoint. The red and brown colouring and the striation of the forms (the paint is actually scratched in places) accentuate the female animality of the nude, which personifies "sexual energy in the raw state, an image of the vital force".[3]

11   Three Figures under a Tree

Trois figures sous un arbre

From the autumn of 1907 to the winter of 1908/09 Picasso, still haunted by the *Demoiselles*, continued to paint very stylized female figures, alone or in groups, inspired by African art. This led to a series of "Bathers in the Forest", to which the present work belongs; these "Bathers" are the synthesis of his efforts to merge rhythm, colour and form and position them in space.

The series begins with the *Nude with Drapery* (1907, Hermitage Museum, St. Petersburg), in which Picasso systematically striates the forms—to define the structure of the nude and to lend a rhythm to the whole—and outlines the volumes in black. The head of the figure has a rhomboid shape.

Another canvas in the series is *Friendship* (1908, Hermitage Museum, St. Petersburg), in which the characteristic features of the subsequent figures are displayed: ochre colouring, drapery over the arm, bodies seen in terms of volume, background

10   *The Nude with Raised Arms*, spring 1908, Paris. Gouache, 32 x 25 cm   ▷

Nude with Drapery, 1907, Hermitage Museum, St. Petersburg

Three Women, 1908, Hermitage Museum, St. Petersburg

Study for "Friendship", 1907/08, Musée Picasso, Paris

with trees, etc. The two figures form a single mass and emerge from the canvas in unison as if they had been hewn out of a single block of wood. They will reappear later in all of the group compositions.

The series continues with groups of bathers and culminates in the winter of 1908/09 with the *Three Women* (1908, Hermitage Museum, St. Petersburg), and the *Dryad* (1908, Hermitage Museum, St. Petersburg). From the dissymmetry of the *Demoiselles* Picasso evolves toward an ever purer geometrization in the spirit of Cézanne. He stops using the decorative African elements (stripes, contrasting colours), but retains the mask-like faces.

In the present work, Picasso creates a rhythm of forms by schematizing the contours: head and nose, breast and shoulders, are defined by broadly echoing lines. The head of the figure on the right merges with that of the middle figure, and numerous other interconnections are evinced. The anatomy is broken up as in the *Demoiselles*, but there is a stronger rhythm here created by the striations and the colours. The three female figures fit one into the other, forming a coherent group.

11 *Three Figures under a Tree*, winter 1907/08, Paris. Oil on canvas, 99 x 99 cm

Cubism

12 Female Head (Fernande)
Tête de femme (Fernande)

Picasso met Fernande Olivier in 1904 in Montmartre, where he then lived, and she would be his companion until 1912.

In the summer of 1909 the couple made a trip to Spain. During their stay in Horta de Ebro, Picasso drew a series of portraits of Fernande that marked the beginning of Analytical Cubism. Back in Paris, Picasso followed the drawings in making a plaster head of Fernande, which Ambroise Vollard later cast in bronze. He applied to the sculpture the principles he had developed in his experiments in two-dimensional representation, where he juxtaposed on a flat surface images of an object seen from different viewpoints. This is the first example of Cubist stylization applied to sculpture.

Study for "Head of Fernande", 1909, Musée Picasso, Paris

Male Head, 1909, Musée Picasso, Paris

Fernande's head is chaotic. The artist has decomposed the hair into bulbous curves, twisted the neck to show both the front and the back, and rendered the features as facets to bring out the internal structure of the face. The light is diffused and syncopated by the interplay of projections and hollows. The forms have been systematized: a similar type of volume is used to represent different parts of the face. In the overall view, the light recomposes the whole.

The structure of the head has however not been negated, it is still traditional in its monolithic aspect; Rodin had disrupted the smoothness of the surface before. This work is of major importance for twentieth-century art because it "introduces discontinuity in the representation of volume".[1] Its example was to be followed by many artists—Archipenko, Laurens, Lipchitz—who tried to transcribe the pictorial language of Cubism into three dimensions.

12 *Female Head (Fernande)*, autumn 1909, Paris. Bronze, 40.5 x 23 x 26 cm

13 Man with a Guitar
Homme à la guitare

This painting displays the characteristic features of Analytical Cubism: grey, brown and ochre colour-scheme, thinly applied paint, fragmentation of the volumes into facets, and geometrization of the planes. It was begun in 1911 and reworked in 1913, as we can see from the inscriptions on the back and from the clearly differentiated stages of the execution. This *Man with a Guitar* is a perfect example of the evolution of Cubism between 1911 and 1913, from the breaking up of the homogeneous form and its integration into the spatial structure to the use of printed letters ("KOU" in the upper right corner) and realistic details (the scrollwork of the chair, the glass) that serve as points of reference. Along with the *Man with a Mandolin*, also in the Picasso Museum, this work is part of a series of monumental paintings from 1911/12 that represent male and female figures with musical instruments. The two pictures in the Picasso Museum are exceptional, however, in that they show the figure full length. In both cases Picasso had to affix an extra

Man with a Mandolin, 1911, Musée Picasso, Paris

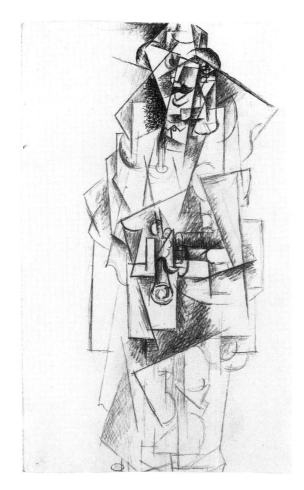

piece of canvas to accommodate the lower part of the body, which looks "unfinished", or at least treated differently from the rest.

The vertical composition and format originated in a drawing.[2] The head is comparable to studies of a mustachioed man with a pipe[3] that present the same treatment of the head as rounded volume. A drawing from 1913[4] displays an identical relationship between the Cubist handling of the figure and the more realistic rendition of the armchair.

Man with a Clarinet, 1911, Musée Picasso, Paris

13 *Man with a Guitar*,
autumn 1911 (1913), Paris.
Oil on canvas, 154 × 77.5 cm

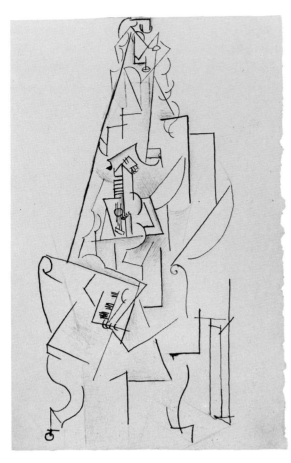

Seated Woman Holding a Guitar, 1912/13, Musée Picasso, Paris

The outstanding feature of this work is the division of the composition into three registers, each of which presents a different tonality and pictorial handling and corresponds to very distinct phases of the development of Cubism. The upper portion with a dark brown ochre tonality shows the fragmentation of the volumes into facets. Picasso later repainted the background so that the contour of the form would stay closed; the man's head seems to stand out against a uniform background and lean heavily toward the front of the painting. In order not to lose touch with reality, so to speak, Picasso preserves the form by enclosing it within its contour. The middle part, painted with light applications of beige and luminous, transparent shimmers, is organized into geometric planes that turn around the centrally-placed hole of the guitar. The instrument is broken up into several elements, thus accommodating itself to the flat structure of the surface. A repetitive graphic rhythm created by the

curved lines and circles and the lined paper suggests movement and music. The orthogonal structure of the planes is counterbalanced by the oblique axes of the guitar and the edge of the table. The bottom part, with a lighter and more simplified handling, seems to be the first statement of a new pictorial language based on a synthetic summarization of the forms of the objects, combined with rectilinear planes and a linear construction. This section is linked to the one above by the lines extending from the corner of the table and the triangle of the sheet of music, but the horizontal separation is still very clearly marked.

The unity of the work comes from the diminution of the figure from the top down, the progressive gain in lightness in both senses of the word. The tension between the object and the flat pictorial space of the background is here greater than ever.

14   Still-Life with Wickerwork Chair
Nature morte à la chaise cannée

The legendary *Still-Life with Wickerwork Chair* marks a turning-point in the history not only of Cubism, but also of twentieth-century art. No wonder that Picasso jealously kept it in his own collection. By introducing, in early 1912, a piece of oilcloth into a picture to represent a chair, Picasso revolutionized the act of painting and called into question centuries of pictorial tradition. Why resort to illusionistic devices with the brush to represent objects when these can be represented by "real" objects? This clearly poses the question of the relationship between art and reality, between the artistic process and mechanical production. But the ambiguity is far from having been resolved here: for one thing, Picasso combines the two systems, and for another, the piece of oilcloth is not real wickerwork, but merely a printed imitation of it. A particular mode of representation is therefore put into practice and called into question at the same time. This confrontation between the two worlds provokes new aesthetic considerations about colour—which is introduced here as an autonomous element—and about the flat area of the piece of oilcloth and its texture, which contrast with the pictorial space and its own materiality.

14 *Still-Life with Wickerwork Chair*, spring 1912, Paris. Oil and printed oilcloth on canvas framed with cord, 29 x 37 cm

In the painted parts we can recognize certain familiar signs: lemon, glass, pipe, knife, scallop, and the stencilled letters "JOU" (for "JOURNAL"). These are the usual elements of the Cubist still-life, the paraphernalia of everyday life, of the bistro table.

The oval format, often used during this period to recentre the composition and contain the energy of the orthogonals, evokes the shape of a table. It is underscored by a false frame made of cord that seems to be a translation into concrete terms of the ornamented pedestal tables represented in many Cubist works. The cord frame also serves to give the painting the status of an object.

Picasso and Braque turned to collage techniques because of their concern for keeping in touch with reality; the logic of Analytical Cubism seemed to be leading to a hermetic impasse. The first step had been the insertion of a nail, then printed letters and imitation materials (wood, sand). Soon after, Braque made the first *papier collé*. The introduction of found materials into a work of art paved the way for the "ready-mades", the assemblages and collages of the Dadaists and the Surrealists.

Collages

15 Violin
Violon

The *Still-Life with Wickerwork Chair* of the spring of 1912 introduced a foreign object into a painting. This decisive step having been taken, the *papier collé*, or collage, now became possible. Braque is said to have invented it in Sorgues in September 1912, when he glued a piece of imitation-wood wallpaper he had spotted in the window of a hardware store onto a charcoal drawing. Soon after, Picasso enthusiastically adopted the technique and made a first series of *papiers collés* in his Boulevard de Raspail studio. "I am using your latest paperistic and dusty (?*pusiéreux*) processes", he wrote to Braque in October 1912.[1] The rationale for this invention was inherent in the logic of Cubism. It was the result of Picasso's and Braque's need for a return to reality and concrete materials after going through the hermetic phase of Analytical Cubism. The *papier collé* permitted a return to colour, which had been neglected since 1907 for the sake of the analysis of forms and their structure; colour could now be applied independently of the form and object represented. Then again, the collage marked the invention of a new system for the representation of reality, in which the artist could play on effects of material and texture, and create a new pictorial space composed of overlapping planes, a way of asserting the two-dimensionality of the picture. As we can see from this *Violin*, relief was only one step away from the flat plane; the *papier collé* imperceptibly becomes a *tableau-relief* by the simple addition of a cardboard box that suggests the volume of the instrument's soundbox and casts a real shadow.

The *Violin* is a synthesis of all of the techniques that Picasso was using at the time—collage, painting and sculpture—abolishing the traditional distinctions between these media. The background is composed of newspaper, as in the *Bottle on a Table*. The use of newspaper is appropriate on several accounts: it is a very ordinary material that is always at hand, it has graphic elements—black lines and printed letters—and the content plays a visual, sometimes symbolic role. The material of the violin is rendered by pieces of imitation-wood wallpaper; the contours and f-holes are drawn in charcoal; the strings are represented by a band of striped paper, and the neck by a piece of paper with painted illusionistic details. The white gouache background adds texture to catch the light. The instrument has been decomposed into its constituent fragments and recomposed in a synthetic and arbitrary fashion by the artist. The witty and playful collages also have a poetic and musical dimension. This example is particularly successful, for it combines with uncompromising simplicity rectilinear planes and curved lines, the dullness of the paper and the luminosity of the white paint.

Bottle on a Table, 1912, Musée Picasso, Paris

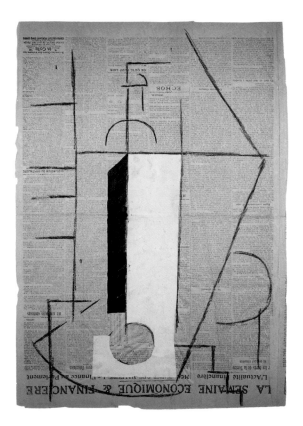

15 *Violin*, 1913/14, Paris. Cardboard box, pasted paper, gouache, charcoal, chalk on cardboard, 51.5 × 30 × 4 cm ▷

16 Guitar

Guitare

In 1913/14 Picasso transposed the principles of the *papiers collés* not only to sculpture (*Glass of Absinth*, pl. 19), but also to painting. The *Guitar* from 1913 looks like a collage, but was in fact done entirely with stencils.

This *Guitar* is doubtless Picasso's most abstract work; if an almost identical collage in which the soundhole is indicated did not exist as well, it would be quite difficult to identify the instrument in the picture. The simple colours and forms—a triangle and rectangles—recall Constructivist works. It was during this crucial period that Mondrian and Malevich were evolving from Cubism to abstraction. Picasso was never to take this path: there is always a representational element in his pictures, no matter how far removed from reality they may seem to be.

Guitar, 1913, Musée Picasso, Paris

Violin and Sheet Music, 1912, Musée Picasso, Paris

17 Glass, Pipe, Ace of Clubs and Die

Verre, pipe, as de trèfle et dé

This *tableau-relief*, or relief-picture, representing a glass, a pipe, a playing-card and a die placed on top of a bistro table, is a good demonstration of the way Picasso, by shifting from the plane to relief, resolved the basic problem of Cubism: how to represent real, three-dimensional objects on a flat surface, how to render volume without resorting to illusionistic perspective, and how to give an overall definition of the object without limiting oneself to a partial view. Picasso uses several techniques simultaneously that he had first developed in his painting before applying them to sculpture. In the same

16 *Guitar*, spring 1913,
Céret. Oil on canvas,
87 x 47.5 cm

Glass, Ace of Clubs, Package of Cigarettes, 1914, Musée Picasso, Paris

work he combines frontal, profile and top views, and even includes real objects in actual relief. The glass is outlined on the left by a simple line on the marbled background, while its curved shape is repeated in blue inside the bas-relief: the right half of the glass is straight, as if its different facets had been unrolled and flattened, then placed one on top of the other, the transparency of the dots permitting their juxtaposition. The bowl of the pipe projects as a cylinder perpendicular to the picture-plane. The playing-card is a piece of metal painted white, with the shape of the ace of clubs cut out. The die is in relief, and adds its four black dots to the *pointillisme* of the background. The tabletop is painted in *trompe-l'œil* fashion to imitate marble, like a real bistro table. These familiar objects of the Cubist still-life rest on a horizontal piece of moulding. The moulded border of the circular piece of wood, probably a found object (stool seat? mirror back?) frames the tondo in the same way as the cord in the *Still-Life with Wickerwork Chair* (pl. 14).

Many *papiers collés* from 1914[2] present different combinations of these same elements: glass, pipe, ace of clubs and die. In one of these works, the fake marble is rendered by a strip of paper; another has a border made of paper printed with imitation wood moulding. The comparison with other techniques enables us to better understand Picasso's visual and conceptual sleight of hand, by which he transforms the elements according to the

mode of expression he has chosen. In the same way that he plays on different viewpoints, Picasso juggles with contrasts of texture and material (wood, metal, paint) and with the various mediums of expression, combining painting and sculpture, representation and realization.

18   Mandolin and Clarinet
Mandoline et clarinette

Mandolin and Clarinet belongs to a series of wood, metal and cardboard constructions or assemblages that Picasso made between 1912 and 1915. Born of the logic inherent in Cubism, of the artist's aspiration toward three-dimensionality, of the extension of pictorial forms into real space, and of the transposition into three dimensions of the idiom and materials of the collage, these constructions represent a major turning-point in twentieth-century sculpture; they paved the way for Constructivism and abstract sculpture. The constructions also integrate what Picasso had learned from African masks, which are also hung on walls and present an architecture of planes and hollows. The subject-matter of the constructions is the same as in the Cubist works: musical instruments and still-life elements.

This construction is composed of a tilted rectangular board that serves to indicate the background plane, two pieces of wood placed vertically and interrupted by two horizontal pieces (the cylindrical one at the bottom represents the clarinet, with black dots for the finger-holes and a disk with concentric circles for the bell). This orthogonal framework is complemented by oblique elements: a triangle at far left, a piece cut in a swallow-tail shape, and a board with a semicircle cut out to suggest the body of the mandolin; the circular piece of wood in the middle stands for its sound-hole. This sculpture composed of intersecting planes cleverly plays on negative space to suggest volume. The use of an unprocessed, homogeneous material, in this case wood, facilitates the laying bare of the architectonic structure, an approach that influenced artists like Tatlin, Gabo and Archipenko.

17 *Glass, Pipe, Ace of Clubs and Die*, 1914, Avignon.
Painted wood and metal elements on a wood support painted in oils, ∅ 34; d. 8.5 cm ▷

Construction: *Bottle of del Mono Anisette and Bowl of Fruit with Grapes*, 1915, Musée Picasso, Paris

Violin and Bottle on a Table, 1915, Musée Picasso, Paris

18 *Mandolin and Clarinet*, 1913, Paris. Deal elements with paint and pencil, 58 x 36 x 23 cm

19 Glass of Absinth
Verre d'absinthe

This is the only bronze sculpture that Picasso executed between 1910 and 1923, and his first "transparent" freestanding sculpture. The glass was first modelled in wax, and Picasso added a real absinth-spoon. It was then cast in six different versions, each painted in different colours. Four have dot-patterns in different places, this one is covered with sand, and the last is painted red and white.

The *Glass of Absinth*, the first "collage-sculpture", is the sculptural synthesis of Picasso's earlier efforts to represent objects without using traditional illusionistic techniques. The glass is shown in its entirety, with base, stem, sides, spoon and sugar. The contours are open, such that the spectator can see the inside and the outside at the same time. Picasso applies the formal innovations that he had experimented with in his constructions, but goes even further by representing an object that is in reality transparent.

The use of a real absinth-spoon with its original function is analogous to the idea behind the *papiers collés*: the introduction of several orders of reality. Werner Spies has distinguished three levels: an element of representation (the glass), an element of reality (the spoon) and an element of imitation (the sugar-cube).[3]

The presence of the absinth-spoon, however, does not mean that the artist intended to produce an illusionistic work. The sand coating on this glass absorbs the light, just as the dot patterns on the other glasses create an imaginary play of light.

There is something anthropomorphic about the bizarre forms that result. We can make out the head of a woman wearing a broad-brimmed hat and a high, close-fitting collar like those worn by women at the turn of the century. This metamorphosis of an object into a human figure is one of the constants of Picasso's art.

Construction: Guitar, 1912, Musée Picasso, Paris

Glass, 1914, Musée Picasso, Paris

19 *Glass of Absinth*, spring 1914, Paris. Painted and sand-covered bronze with absinth-spoon, 21.5 x 16.5 x 6.5 cm
(On loan from Musée National d'Art Moderne, Centre Georges Pompidou)

20 Violin
Violon

This *Violin* from 1915 is derived from the work on the *papiers collés*, from compositions of overlapping coloured planes. It is the culmination in relief of Synthetic Cubism, which reduces objects to rectilinear, geometric planes that reveal their formal structure, their abstract architecture, rather than their anecdotal particularities. Around 1915 Picasso abandoned the decorative style of so-called Rococo Cubism in favour of a more geometric and rigorous idiom, which we can see in the *Harlequin* (The Museum of Modern Art, New York) and the *Man in front of a Fireplace* (Musée Picasso, Paris). The violin is identifiable as such thanks to the f-holes indicated by two long, hollow brown rectangles. This type of sculpture with open, cut-out forms and reversed volumes was inaugurated in 1912 with the famous *Guitar* (The Museum of Modern Art, New York), which was first made out of cardboard, then metal. Folding is a characteristic

Guitar, 1924, Musée Picasso, Paris

Bottle of Bass, Glass and Newspaper, 1914, Musée Picasso, Paris

common to Picasso's works in cardboard and in metal. Flat sheets of metal are folded to create negative volumes that integrate real space and suggest relief. The wood constructions emphasize the assemblage of different elements. The more homogeneous ones in metal lay bare the internal structure of the objects, and as such are closer to the paintings. These constructions break away from the closed volume of free-standing sculpture, thereby paving the way for Constructivism. But they are different from the works of Picasso's Russian counterparts (Tatlin, Rodchenko) in that they still acknowledge the plane of the wall by their frontality, and thus remain pictorial, while their painted surface negates the specificity of the materials. Picasso executed other sculptures in painted sheet-metal: *Bottle of Bass, Glass and Newspaper* (1914) and *Guitar* (1924), both in the Picasso Museum.

20   *Violin*, 1915, Paris. Cut, folded and painted sheet-metal, wire, 100 x 63.7 x 18 cm   ▷

Return to Representation

21 The Painter and His Model
Le peintre et son modèle

Picasso's sojourn in Avignon in June 1914 co-incided with his return to naturalism. The works from this period anticipate the classical revival of the early twenties.

We see the painter and his model in the studio, indicated by a palette and a canvas on an easel. The painter is seated, resting his head on his hand in a pose that recalls Cézanne's *Smoker* (Pushkin Museum, Moscow) or the *Man Seated at a Table*, a 1914 drawing in the Picasso Museum. He is look-ing at the model, Eva Gouel, his mistress, who died the following year. This is the only known portrait of her, which perhaps explains why it was never publicly shown during the painter's lifetime.

This was the year in which Picasso was working on the integration of objects into his works without changing their original function—the spoon in the *Glass of Absinth* (pl. 19), for example. In the pres-ent work, the same principle led the artist to include an illusionistic element in a room where other motifs—a chair, a table, a bowl of fruit, a painter

(Picasso himself?)—are simply sketched. The model, however, is the only motif *painted* in a naturalistic manner during this period. The artist's return to verisimilitude may be seen in his pencilled portraits of Max Jacob and Ambroise Vollard.

Pierre Daix writes that "Picasso had learned from Cubism that it was enough to give essential indica-tions of the object or figure to help the spectator make a mental, or 'conceptual', image of it".[1] Be-cause it was deliberately left unfinished, this canvas (in fact a kitchen towel, as the red stripes show) is easy to read at a glance. Had it been finished, the eye would have got lost in it, as it often does in traditional painting. The artist does not use classi-cal perspective to give the illusion of depth: he en-larges the hands and legs to bring them closer to the spectator, and the painted model stands out from the picture plane. The painter's legs hide those of his chair, and the placing of the table legs seems illogical.

Picasso had a particular affinity with the subject of the painter and his model in a studio. He often represented it, treating it according to the pictorial idiom of the moment. There is nothing gratuitous about the choice of subject-matter here. In repre-senting his own activity as an artist, Picasso is pro-claiming a manifesto: "By reintroducing resem-blance, Picasso intended above all to do away with the finishing and filling-in inherent in traditional painting. Using illusionistic techniques, he reinstat-ed the concentration of the gaze that Cubist figura-tion had permitted. He demonstrated that he could assert or deny resemblance at will, without jeop-ardising the coherence of the composition."[2]

Man Seated at a Table, 1914, Musée Picasso, Paris

21 *The Painter and His Model*, summer 1914, Avignon. Oil and pencil on canvas, 58 x 55.9 cm

22 Portrait of Olga in an Armchair
Portrait d'Olga dans un fauteuil

Picasso met Olga Kokhlova, a dancer in the Ballets Russes, during the trip he made to Italy in 1917 with Jean Cocteau to put the finishing touches to his sets for *Parade*. This is the first known portrait of his future wife. It was executed in his studio in Montrouge after a photograph and a pose studied in a drawing, and, judging by the photograph, it is a good likeness. It has often been said that his marriage in 1918 to Olga, the daughter of a Russian general and a quite proper young society lady, coincided with the Cubist revolutionary's return to orthodoxy and the beginning of his classical period in the twenties, with the attendant change of lifestyle. While there is no doubt that Olga's social ambitions, the couple's frequentation of ballet society, and his new art-dealer Paul Rosenberg played a major role in his new way of life, these factors in no way determined his change of style. The return to naturalistic representation dates back to 1914; and if one looks more closely, there is

Study for "Portrait of Olga in an Armchair", 1917, artist's estate

nothing very classical about this portrait, which appears on the face of it to be in the great tradition of Ingres. The conventional treatment is combined with features derived from Cubism: the deliberately unfinished armchair and the crudely sketched neutral, empty background are in opposition to the purity of the line and the careful rendering of the details, especially the sheerness of the dress, the flower-patterns, and the fan and jewellery. The figure itself seems to have been cut out and pasted onto the background, from which it is separated by rough shading. The armchair and its decorative floral designs are handled like a collage of printed wallpaper, and it stands in the same plane as the figure of Olga. This juxtaposition of different spaces—the flatness of the background and the armchair, the illusionistic space of the figure—is typical of the dual spatial registers that Picasso created in his painting during this period. Olga's somewhat bland beauty, her finely drawn features, thin mouth, refined elegance and distinction are enlivened by Picasso's unorthodox treatment. Except when she is represented as a mother, the dreamy-eyed and somewhat sad-looking Olga inspired rather cold and distant portraits that are no doubt revelatory of the state of their marriage.

Olga in the Studio at Montrouge, 1917, photograph by Picasso, Picasso Archives

22 *Portrait of Olga in an Armchair,* winter 1917, Montrouge. Oil on canvas, 130 x 88.8 cm ▷

23 The Bathers

Les baigneuses

From 1918 onward, Picasso spent all of his summers at the seashore, first at Biarritz, then on the
Côte d'Azur or in Dinard. These sojourns inspired
the creation of a new series of works on the theme
of bathers. This small picture painted in 1918 in
Biarritz, where the newlyweds were summering as
the guests of Madame Errazuriz, was the first of the
series. The theme of female nudity associated with
the sea has a long tradition, extending from Bot-
ticelli's *Venus* to Cézanne's *Bathers*. Here, though,
there is the additional allusion to the recently-intro-
duced fashion of sea bathing, to which Picasso,
with his Mediterranean origins, enthusiastically
subscribed. A contemporary drawing of bathers[3]
gives an idea of the healthy, active life of vacation-
ers on sunny beaches, free of cumbersome clothing
and cares.

 Although of modest dimensions, the painting
gives an impression of monumentality. It condenses a number of pictorial references: Seurat's views
of Port-en-Bessin (lighthouse, breakwater, horizontal bands of sea and sky), Italian Mannerism (elongated bodies, smooth and precise handling, sharp
colours), Rousseau's primitivism (schematization
and geometrization of forms, realistic and minutely-
rendered details), Derain's "Gothic" style, and
above all Ingres (in particular the *Turkish Bath*).
Picasso's interpretation of Ingres during this period
is much more radical than in earlier works; he takes
the "deformer's" lessons to their ultimate consequences, thus "liberating Ingres from his Raphael
complex":[4] elongation of the bodies and a freedom of line that forces the anatomy to bend itself to
pictorial rhythms, to plays of curves and arabesques. The step from deformation to monstrosity,
already suggested by Ingres, found a ready response in Picasso, who subsequently submitted the
female body to every imaginable metamorphosis.
These anatomical deformations—here relatively
innocuous—are related to his studies of dancers at
the Ballets Russes, which he often frequented at the
time.

 This canvas, which Picasso kept for his own reference, occupies a special place in his work: the de-

Bather, 1918, Fogg Art Museum, Cambridge

tailed realism, the simple and direct handling, the
sinuous grace of the lean and lithe bodies are rare
features—Picasso usually portrays more gener-
ously-endowed female anatomies.

 The transparency of the light notwithstanding,
these prosaic modern Venuses in their clinging
swimsuits, the biomorphic forms of the rocks and
pebbles, the stillness of the sea, the frozen gestures
of the bathers, and the ecstatic attitude of the
standing woman with her tentacular hair produce
an overall impression of strangeness and menace,
a surrealistic atmosphere comparable to certain
seascapes by Tanguy, or to the series of "Bathers"
painted at Dinard in 1928 and 1929.

J.B. Ingres, *Turkish Bath*, 1859–1863, Musée du Louvre,
Paris

23 *The Bathers*, summer 1918, Biarritz. Oil on canvas, 27 x 22 cm

The Neoclassical Period

24 Still-Life with Pitcher and Apples
Nature morte au pichet et aux pommes

This still-life was discovered only after the painter's death. The composition is extremely simple—four apples, a pitcher, a plate—without any decor or personalized objects. It alludes to no season and to no particular place, and this gives it a universal character. The arrangement of the objects makes no practical sense: two apples on the sideboard on either side of a pitcher, on top of which is a plate with two more apples.

The rusticality and simplicity of this still-life contrasts with the abundance to which art history has accustomed us. The chalky colours—grey and beige—recall frescoes in Pompeii and Herculaneum. Picasso probably visited these sites during his trip to Rome in 1917.

With these simple forms and the monumentality of the pitcher in the middle (a frequently recurring object in his paintings), Picasso was fully in line with the return to classicism then in vogue. In front of this silent composition, it is impossible not to think of the metaphysical still-lifes of Morandi.

Nevertheless, there is something disquieting here. Against the neutral background, the pitcher may also be seen as a female figure with generous forms: with her voluptuously open mouth and the generous swelling of the highlighted belly, this pitcher-woman is as erotic and colossal as the giantesses painted during the same period.

Picasso again uses a classical idiom and interprets it in his own way. The elaboration of the composition shows a very Cézannesque handling enriched by the Cubist experience. The image of a woman's body, which emerges where no one would have expected it, has not been downplayed; on the contrary, it is overwhelmingly present and sensual. Picasso also represented the metaphor of the woman-as-object in such works as the *Glass of Absinth* of 1914 (pl. 19) and the *Straw Hat with Blue Foliage* of 1936 (pl. 67).

Still-Life on a Dresser, 1919, Musée Picasso, Paris

24 *Still-Life with Pitcher and Apples*, 1919. Oil on canvas, 65 x 43 cm

25 Seated Woman
Femme assise

The heavy, powerfully modelled features of this *Seated Woman* attest to Picasso's interest in monumental Roman statuary. Throughout the series of colossal women painted during the period from 1920 to 1923, we find the same large, vacuous, evenly drawn eyes, with the line of the nose extending the eyebrows: "Junos with cow-like eyes and great, square hands that hold drapery made of stone."[1]

The white garment is also a reference to antiquity, but—along the lines of the tablecloths in Cézanne's still-lifes—the drapery here becomes stone-like and takes on the same consistency as the body. This unusual type of modelling creates an ambiguous form suggestive of sculpture. Picasso gives these giantesses the solidity and weight of statues, and plays on their proportions in order to accentuate their monumental appearance: the hands and feet are too big for the bodies. Here, the woman's body is compressed into virtually a parallelogram, resting solidly on the broad pedestal of the four-toed foot. The nonchalant gesture of the fingers recalls poses by Ingres, except that here sensuality has given way to a ponderous, frozen revery devoid of all expressivity.

These distortions and exaggerated proportions

Girl with Bare Feet, 1895, Musée Picasso, Paris

are of course part of a symbolic image of woman, but they also serve a purely pictorial purpose. Picasso wants to show as much as possible of the reality he perceives. During his Cubist days, he would lay out all the facets of an object and represent multiple viewpoints in order to conduct an analysis, and later a synthesis, of its formal specificity, its internal structure. But in this work he uses another method: confident in his new freedom, and conscious of the reality of the painting as an object, he deploys the limbs fulsomely on the flat surface of the canvas, so that they all have the same value, the same solidity, and fully occupy the pictorial space.

Picasso was particularly fond of the theme of the seated woman, or woman in an armchair, and represented it throughout his career in many different manners. The first example was the still and pensive *Girl with Bare Feet* (1895).

Female Head, 1921, Musée Picasso, Paris

25 *Seated Woman*, 1920, Paris. Oil on canvas, 92 x 65 cm ▷

26 Reading the Letter
La lecture de la lettre

The faces of these two friends may also be seen in *The Pipes of Pan* of 1923 (pl. 30), where there is a similar treatment of the heavy, square-cut hands, and a similar pensive mood that seems to unite the two figures in a common meditation. "This most enigmatic of pictures, *Reading the Letter*, is close to Courbet's realism in the rendition of the costumes, and has a Michelangelesque feeling in the volumes. It is a coded picture, which very likely alludes to one of Picasso's friendships—with the poet Apollinaire? with Braque, the painter with whom he shared the Cubist adventure? The bowler hat in the foreground can be seen in the portraits of Apollinaire and Braque, while the books and the letter are attributes of poetry and writing."[2]

The Apollinaire hypothesis seems plausible, for it was also in 1921 that Picasso painted *The Three Musicians* (The Museum of Modern Art, New York), which may be seen as the pictorial testament of Cubism and as a spiritual testament; the figures represent Picasso, Apollinaire and Max Jacob. In the same year, the committee to raise a statue to Guillaume Apollinaire met for the first time under the chairmanship of Serge Pérat.[3] The hat, which is sometimes called "the Cronstadt" or "Cézanne's hat",[4] is an allusion to Cubism and to a still-life from 1909.[5] The picture also expresses a community of spirit in the renewal of classicism: Apollinaire's influence on the return to classical inspiration[6] was at least as important, if not more so, than Cocteau's. As the poet himself wrote: "I am trying to renew the poetic style, but in a classical style", and, speaking of his head-wound, "a splendid Minerva was born of my brain". The theme of male friendship, already treated in the Gósol *Adolescents* of 1906 (National Gallery of Art, Washington D.C.), and taken up again in these two pictures from 1921 and 1923, may be difficult to interpret, but it is no doubt an indication of Picasso's deep and loyal feelings for his friends.

The Hat, 1909, private collection, Switzerland

26 *Reading the Letter*, 1921, Paris. Oil on canvas, 184 x 105 cm ▷

27 Three Women at the Fountain
Trois femmes à la fontaine

The series of gigantic and monumental women dates from the years 1918 to 1924, the period when Picasso returned to the classical tradition. He was not the only one: other artists, such as Matisse, Braque and Léger, also turned to more classical forms after the war.

At the same time Picasso was pursuing his experiments in Synthetic Cubism, which culminated in the two versions of *The Three Musicians* (The Museum of Modern Art, New York; Philadelphia Museum of Art), both painted in 1921, the same year as these *Three Women at the Fountain*, which has been described by one author as being "the purest example of Picasso's Neoclassical style".[7] Preceded by nine studies, the subject was treated in two slightly different versions; the second one, painted in oil, is in New York (The Museum of Museum of Modern Art).

The composition is rigorously constructed on an orthogonal axis cut by a diagonal. The three hieratic figures are disposed in a semicircle around the focal point: the earthenware jug. The movements of the arms and the different stances of the figures create a continuous arabesque within an enclosed space. There are no details to connect these creatures to the real world; they are beyond time.

Their monolithic, statuesque appearance immediately brings the sculptures of the Parthenon to mind. "Not only did he clothe his women in an-

tique-style tunics, but he also included all sorts of referential signs",[8] such as the drapery with straight folds, the aquiline noses elongating the forehead, the hair rolled up or gathered in buns.

This return to Mediterranean imagery is linked to a very happy period in the artist's life. Picasso was a father, Olga having given birth to their son Paulo in February, and he had rented a villa at Fontainebleau for the summer. The name of the town probably inspired the title of the picture, and possibly also that of *The Spring*.

The Spring, 1921, Musée Picasso, Paris

Study of a Hand for "Three Women at the Fountain", 1921, Musée Picasso, Paris

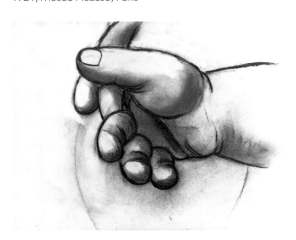

Study for "Three Women at the Fountain", 1921, Musée Picasso, Paris

27 *Three Women at the Fountain*, summer 1921, Fountainebleau. Red chalk on canvas, 200 x 161 cm

While Picasso's antique inspiration is evident here, there are other historical sources: Michelangelo's *Sybils* in Rome (which Picasso visited in 1917) appear proportionately every bit as colossal, and the serenity of the scene recalls Poussin's *Et in Arcadia Ego* (c. 1650, Musée du Louvre, Paris). The three women have the same classical "remoteness" as Poussin's shepherds, but without the idealized landscape.

Picasso transcribes the classical models into his own idiom: these gigantic women, whose globular eyes recall those of 1906/07, are a further step in his deformation of the human figure.

28 Family at the Seaside
Famille au bord de la mer

The mysterious and poetic *Family at the Seaside*, small in format yet so monumental in feeling, may be interpreted as an image of fatherhood. These three figures by the sea probably represent Olga, Picasso and their son Paulo (born in 1921). The family group forms a triangle, with the young father as the base, and the watchful and protective head of the mother at the apex. The woman seems to be protecting not only the child, but the father too, who is represented asleep, lost to the world, modestly covering his genitals with his hand. The gesture of the child symbolically putting his finger in his father's ear is reinforced by the mother's arm. All the bonds of the flesh are reformulated here, pointing to procreation.

This unusual depiction of the family, for which there are a number of preparatory sketches,[9] may be compared to the representation of *Motherhood* of the previous year (The Art Institute of Chicago). Yet it is far removed from the traditional, classical versions of the theme that Picasso painted during this period, even if submission to the triumphant, nourishing mother remains a persistent feature. The position of the figures in the present work recalls a recurrent theme in Picasso's work, the "sleep-watcher"—except that here it is the man who sleeps and the woman who watches. Considering all the antique elements, this could also be a representation of Ulysses cast ashore and discovered by Nausicaa.

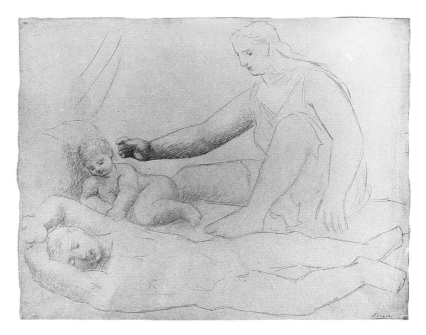

Study for "Family at the Seaside", 1922, Musée Picasso, Paris

Two Bathers, 1921, Musée Picasso, Paris

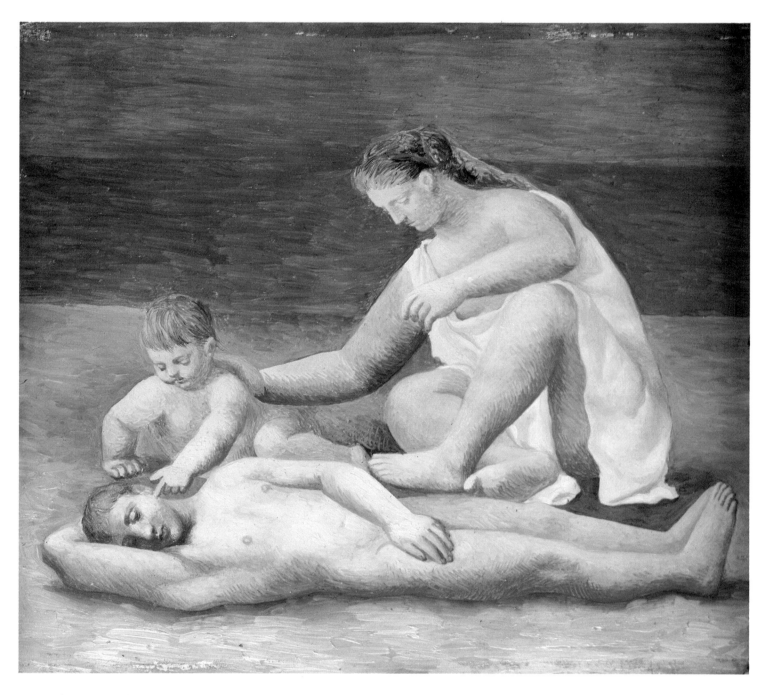

28 *Family at the Seaside*, summer, 1922, Dinard. Oil on wood, 17.6 x 20.2 cm

29 Two Women Running on the Beach (The Race)

Deux femmes courant sur la plage (La course)

The visual shock of this frenetic work comes from the contrast between the weight of the statuesque amazons and the lightness of their movements. Despite the heaviness of their massive limbs, they seem to be carried away by the momentum of the race and about to take off. The contradictoriness of the impressions created boosts the tension and the energy that propels the two bodies through space. In order to suggest this dynamism, Picasso uses a variety of formal devices: flowing clothes and hair, the head of the nearer figure thrown back like the goddess in Ingres's *Jupiter and Thetis* (Musée Granet, Aix-en-Provence) or one of the figures in the Biarritz *Bathers* from 1918 (pl. 23), the other figure's averted face, the robustness of the bodies, and the strong diagonals and horizontals that scan the composition. The idea of upward motion is expressed by the triangle formed by the obliques of the arms; the arm thrust forward, extending the axis of the back leg, gives an impression of extreme elongation and speed.

Not surprisingly, Picasso chose this gouache for the design of the stage curtain for Diaghilev's ballet *The Blue Train* (1924), which was performed to the music of Darius Milhaud and a text by Jean Cocteau. The action of the ballet takes place at a fashionable seaside resort and celebrates the healthy and active outdoor life.

This work shows how Picasso uses classicism for his own purposes, overturning the canons of traditional figuration: the perspective is reversed (the hand in the left foreground is smaller than the more distant one on the right), proportions are ignored, and the left breasts are strangely placed. Pierre Daix rightly qualifies this as *classicisme piégé*, "manipulated classicism". The Cubist experience combined with the example of Ingres gave Picasso complete freedom in his figural representation, which he later pushed to the extreme in his *Metamorphoses*.

The Bather, 1921, private collection

29 *Two Women Running on the Beach (The Race)*, summer 1922, Dinard. Gouache on plywood, 32.5 x 41.1 cm

30 The Pipes of Pan
La flûte de Pan

This painting, which is unanimously recognized as the masterpiece of the Neoclassical Period, must have represented a milestone for Picasso too, for it never left his studio. The grandeur, simplicity and nobility of the composition and its profoundly Mediterranean character have often been commented upon. "Two young shepherds or fishermen with massive and powerfully modelled forms stand by the sea, in an ostensibly Mediterranean decor. The seated musician is absorbed in his playing, while his companion stands pensively, resting his weight on one leg. The composition is balanced by the contrast between these two typical poses of Western art. Through a humanist tradition that extends from Cézanne back to Giotto and to the pediments of Olympia, Picasso revives the world of noble rusticality and harmonious fullness on which we nostalgically dwell."[11]

Reverdy saw in this work the application of the golden rule of classicism, the subordination of the parts to the whole. "No pose or gesture should be anything else but the formal perfection of the means used. No head, body or arm that is not in its place, each element contributing to the effect of the whole. No other meaning beyond the plastic constitution of the picture."[12]

The influences and sources for this painting have been retraced in great detail: Cézanne's *Bathers* (The Museum of Modern Art, New York), Perugino's *Apollo and Marsyas*, the Pompeian fresco *Pan and the Nymphs*, the sculpted group of *Pan and Daphnis* in the Naples museum. André Fermigier, however, notes that "these antique reminiscences notwithstanding, the atmosphere in this painting is evidently not the same as that of a classical idyll or pastoral. Tityrus and Moelibeus are represented here as two peasant-youths, two young fishermen with powerful but graceless bodies and disproportioned hands and feet. They are clothed not in artistically arranged drapery, but in rather unaesthetic bathing-trunks that further accentuate their commonness. There is no idealization in this work. We might identify 'cubistic' elements in the treatment of the limbs, but that is not

the point. One is reminded not so much of Michelangelo's athletes as of Cézanne's bathers. *The Pipes of Pan* is in fact the most Cézannesque picture that Picasso ever painted. Here is indeed a 'Poussin done after nature', a 1923 Cézanne of the best vintage. The balance between the nobility of the vision and the sincerity of the observation of crude reality amply justifies the comparison of this work to those of the Aix master."[13]

There exist a number of drawings from 1923 that show curly-haired Grecian-type youths playing pastoral instruments, sitting alone on a pedestal or accompanied by female figures.

The most disquieting element of this composition is probably the background, which is formed of cubes and large vertical panels that frame the horizontal expanse of the sea and sky. The space so created, which looks like a stage-set, tends to close the figures in, gives an impression of depth, and contrasts with the sculptural quality of the bodies. This type of abstract, geometric and completely artificial background is fairly rare in Picasso's work during this period: the "Bathers" from the same year are all represented in a naturalistic setting. There is every reason to believe that the scene is

Youth with a Mirror, Nude, Flute Player and Child, 1923, private collection

30 *The Pipes of Pan*, summer 1923, Antibes. Oil on canvas, 205 x 174 cm not simply an evocation of antiquity, and that the two figures in the imaginary, theatrical decor might be friends of Picasso's connected with his Neoclassical inspiration. Other male couples symbolizing friendship may be seen in *Reading the Letter* (pl. 26) and in *The Adolescents* from the Gósol period.

31   Paulo as Harlequin
Paul en arlequin

Picasso had a special fondness for the theme of childhood, which occupied him from his Blue Period (*Child with a Dove*, 1901, Tate Gallery, London) to the end of his career (*Young Painter*, 1972, Musée Picasso, Paris); he often portrayed his own children—Paulo, Maya, later Claude and Paloma. Like Goya, Reynolds and Renoir, he sought to express all the dimensions of childhood and the emotions it inspired: tenderness, fragility, innocence, revery, play.

   This portrait of the three-year-old Paulo in the diamond-patterned costume of Harlequin belongs to a series of portraits, two others of which are in the Picasso Museum: *Paulo Drawing* and *Paulo Dressed as Pierrot*. The unfinished painting, in which a *pentimento* is discernible, recalls the *Portrait of Olga in an Armchair* (pl. 22): there is the

Paulo Dressed as Pierrot, 1925, Musée Picasso, Paris

Paulo Drawing, 1923, Musée Picasso, Paris

same neutral greyish-beige background, the precision of detail, the armchair. The Harlequin theme is an important one in Picasso's work, and so it is tempting to interpret this picture as an idealized projection of the father onto the son; the dark eyes with which the boy gazes fixedly are those of the artist. Paulo's fragility and unreality are accentuated by the instability of his pose. Although one leg is slightly bent under, he is really neither leaning against the armchair nor sitting on it, like Olga in the 1917 portrait. He seems to have been set against the dark form of the chair like a playing-card, and in this respect recalls Manet's *Fife-Player*. The figure floats like an apparition, its feet not painted in, although the first version of the pose, which is still visible, would have shown him standing squarely on his feet.

   Because of the smooth and porcelain-like handling and the delicacy of the details, which display Picasso's mastery of the classical style during this period, the picture deserves to be ranked among such masterpieces as Goya's portraits of the royal children.

31   *Paulo as Harlequin*, 1924, Paris, Oil on canvas, 130 × 97.5 cm   ▷

On the Fringes of Surrealism I

32 The Kiss
Le baiser

This enigmatic picture was virtually unknown before the painter's death, and has often been the subject of erroneous interpretations. Zervos[1] titled it *Seated Woman*, the catalogue of the 1953 exhibition in Rome[2] *On the Beach*. These divergent readings—indoor scene, outdoor scene—are evidence of the picture's hermeticism and of the perceptual block that has kept critics from identifying its real subject. Exceptional also in its anticipatory style, the importance of *The Kiss* equals that of *The Dance* in the Tate Gallery, painted a short time before, in June 1925. *The Kiss* is a product of the summer holiday Picasso spent in Juan-les-Pins with Olga and Paulo. Both the place and the time have their importance in its conception.

The year 1925 marked a break in Picasso's style. This painting has the same aggressivity and gives the same visual shock as *The Dance*, which displays similar formal features. In both works the flat shapes are exploded, dislocated and freely reassembled like parts of a puzzle, and there are exaggerations, deformations, an interweaving of the planes and motifs, of illusionistic and cubistic space, and a strident colour-scheme.

The new style was associated with the appearance of Surrealism, which preached the liberation of the instincts, and whose motto was: "Beauty will either be convulsive or not at all". It also coincided with marital tensions and conflicts between Picasso and Olga, which led the artist to give vent to violence and aggression in his representations of women.

Juan-les-Pins, where Picasso spent the summers 1920, 1924, 1925 and 1926, saw the beginning of a very distinct and little-studied period in his work, inaugurated by a small landscape from 1920 (Musée Picasso, Paris). The characteristic features of this period may be seen in the famous "ab-

stract" sketchbook, in which the drawings are composed of dots and lines, in several large still-lifes (*Mandolin and Guitar*, 1924, Guggenheim Museum, New York; *Studio with Plaster Head*, 1925, The Museum of Modern Art, New York), and in the present work. *The Kiss* should be considered in this particular context; we need only compare it with two drawings in the Juan-les-Pins sketchbook from 1925 to understand its sources and pictorial language. These implicit references explain why Venturi, in his preface to the 1953 catalogue, adopted the title *On the Beach*, which Picasso apparently did not dispute; nobody saw here the evocation of a kiss. Yet how can we not see in this veritable explosion of forms and colours the representation of a man and a woman in a stormy embrace? Picasso does nothing to facilitate its reading: the bodies are completely intermingled, limbs and organs are upside-down, a multitude of techniques have been marshalled to express erotic frenzy, attraction and repulsion, and above all the complete fusion of two beings in an embrace.

View of Juan-les-Pins, 1920, Musée Picasso, Paris

32 *The Kiss*, summer, 1925, Juan-les-Pins. Oil on canvas, 130.5 x 97.7 cm

Page from a sketchbook, 1925, Musée Picasso, Paris

On the left we can identify the figure of the man, his target-like eye and his phallus-shaped nose. The mouth, which can also be read as an eye and a woman's sex, is common to both figures, which seem to be welded together by a pattern of horizontal bars and interpenetrating organs. The woman's head is thrown backward and is shown both in profile and from above. The man clasps her with one arm in a vice-like grip around her neck, and with the other seems to be pinning her arms behind her back. This would explain the position of the woman's arm, which is painted red, while the pink, hairy arm belongs to the man. The woman is com-

The Kiss, 1929, Musée Picasso, Paris

Page from a sketchbook, 1925, Musée Picasso, Paris

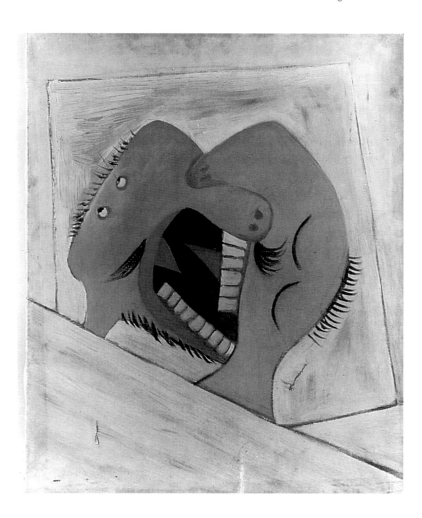

The Kiss, 1931, Musée Picasso, Paris

pletely wedged in: on the left by a brown leg with a pattern like corrugated cardboard and a white foot, in the bottom right corner by the sole of a hobnailed boot. The woman's feet seem to be lifted off the ground, the toes spread in ecstasy or in her effort to resist. The nail-like treatment of the toes and of the black, bell-shaped breast in the man's clutches recalls *The Dance* and other pictures from this period. At the bottom of the canvas there is a strange sign that could be read as a sun, a vulva or an anus, also found in the small nudes painted at Boisgeloup in the thirties. It could be seen as a prefiguration of Georges Bataille's *anus solaire*.

The grid-pattern in the centre may be interpreted as the woman's dress, or as a Cubist pictorial device used to suggest transparency; it can be seen in most of the drawings in the sketchbooks from

Juan-les-Pins. On another level it expresses the symbolic network of bonds that join man and woman in their embrace. Rosenblum[3] identifies specific formal elements as clothing and furniture and interprets the scene as a representation of the conflict between instinctive urges and the fetters of the modern environment, the spontaneity of desire coming up against vestimentary obstacles, and also as an expression of the conflict between Picasso and Olga.

It should not be forgotten that this pictorial language, derived from the abstract point-and-line drawings, is related to that of "automatic writing", and that some of the forms are purely random.

This provocative picture demonstrates Picasso's aggressive and anarchic humour, not to say barbarism. No wonder it rarely left his studio.

33 Guitar
Guitare

This is one of Picasso's most powerful and irreducible works, not just for its formal and technical innovations, but also for the malefic forces that seem to be at work. It has a pendant in another guitar (right) of similar inspiration, in which the nails are stuck into the support from the front; here they are driven in from the back and protrude aggressively. The sordidness of the soiled and torn rag, pierced with a hole, the pieces of string that pass through the canvas, the nails, all make for an impression of malaise, of pain, and give both works an aura of "sacred horror".[4] In the words of Roland Penrose: "The cruel shock of this work is not relieved by any decorative lines or the charms of colour. It is an expression of strong and aggressive anger in a language that makes it painfully clear."[5] In order to underscore the sadistic aspect of this "mean" art, Picasso at one point considered inserting razor-blades in the corners so as to make it that much more untouchable.

Around this time Picasso used similar materials and techniques in a series of small guitars made of cardboard, pieces of tulle, string and nails. They are pictured on a page of one of the sketchbooks,

Guitar, 1926, Musée Picasso, Paris

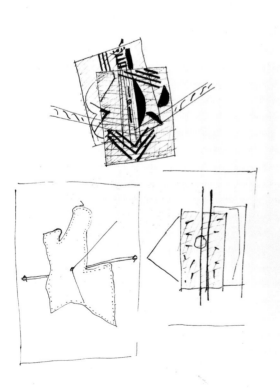

and they would seem to confirm the vertical orientation of the present work (the cord and nail seem to indicate that it should be hung horizontally). While the composition of this *Guitar* and the presence of a piece of newspaper recall the Cubist guitars and *papiers collés*, the spirit and the technical realization are quite different here. It is no longer a matter of collage but of assemblage, and the found materials are used as they are, more for their suggestive power than for their specific formal qualities. This rehabilitation of discarded objects and integration of everyday reality into the artistic sphere was part of the Surrealist programme: to bridge the gulf between art and life and disrupt aesthetic vision through unexpected associations. The dramatic character of the work did not escape

Page from a sketchbook, 1926, artist's estate

33 *Guitar*, spring 1926, Paris. String, newspaper, floorcloth and nails on painted canvas, 130 x 96 cm the notice of the Surrealists, who duly reproduced it in the Journal *La révolution surréaliste* in 1926.

The use of nails here is only distantly related to the *trompe-l'œil* nails in some Cubist works. They are not only symbols of aggression and sexual metaphors, but also magic weapons. Their placement and number recall certain nail-studded tribal fetish-objects as well as the voodoo practice of sticking pins into figurines or attributes to cast spells on people. Lydia Gasman[6] has interpreted the two guitars as the expression of the struggle between two antagonistic forces: between Destiny or Death and Picasso himself. Given Picasso's fetishism and his superstition about clothes, not to mention the conflicts in his marriage at the time, it would be tempting to go along with Gasman's interpretation that the other *Guitar* is Picasso's own "crucifixion", for he used his own shirt in it, and that the one presented here is a death-wish directed at Olga, who is symbolized by a domestic attribute, the wash-rag. The enigmatic and magical dimension of these disturbing works is confirmed by Picasso's own statements and by the fact that he never parted with them. In an interview with Carlton Lake[7] he referred to the connection between this guitar and the cave paintings of Lascaux and Altamira.

Some of Picasso's poetic texts[8] also allude to the symbolic significance of nails: "The nails of fate are blindly driven into the body"; "the handkerchief nailed to the window"; "these crucified rags".

34 The Painter and His Model
Le peintre et son modèle

This large painting all in grey and white was the starting point for a long series of thematic and stylistic variations. It is contemporary with another large monochromatic grey composition, *The Dressmaker's Workshop* (Musée National d'Art Moderne, Paris), in which the pattern of rounded forms could be seen as the "positive" counterpoint of the present work, which inaugurated what came

Page from a sketchbook, 1925/26, Musée Picasso, Paris

The Dressmaker's Workshop, 1926, Musée National d'Art Moderne, Paris

34   *The Painter and His Model*, 1926, Paris. Oil on canvas, 172 x 256 cm

*Illustration for Balzac's
"Unknown Masterpiece"*, 1927,
Musée Picasso, Paris

to be called "Curvilinear Cubism". In this style, the figures are built up out of a network of constantly intertwining curved lines, not unlike the randomly traced forms of "automatic writing", in which the pencil is left to itself, unguided by conscious control. Picasso used a similar pictorial idiom in the drawings he made about this time as illustrations to Balzac's *Unknown Masterpiece*. One of these drawings shows the painter and a seated woman who knits while he covers the canvas with a tangle of lines. The network of interconnected lines in the present work expresses the complex ties between the painter and his model. There is also a direct allusion to Frenhofer's picture in *The Unknown Masterpiece*, as the only identifiable element in the confused mass of forms is a foot.

The painter and his model is one of the major themes in Picasso's work. First documented in 1914 (pl. 21), it is developed in the series of "Studios" of 1927/28 and in the *Vollard Suite*, and culminates in a series devoted to the subject in the sixties. It is a rich subject, for it confronts man with woman, the objective with the desiring eye, art with life; it is the symbolic representation of the act of creation.

The artist is easily identifiable on the right with his palette, but his head is doubled and his features are completely disorganized, especially the eyes. The woman on the left has been reduced to a tiny head, a long neck, hands of unequal size and an enormous foot, prefigurations of the organic metamorphoses and permutations to come. In the background we can see the side of the canvas, indicated by a line of nails, and a small picture representing a black-and-white "lunar" head in the manner characteristic of this period. Picasso here inaugurates his extreme transformations of the female body, changing its proportions through striking inversions of perspective. There is a condensed example of the procedure in the 1927 *Figure* (Musée Picasso, Paris). The network of arabesques stands out against a flat pattern of grey areas which, like the *papiers collés* of the decade before, serve to suggest depth and emphasize the picture plane.

35 Guitar

Guitare

On 12 June 1912 Picasso wrote to Kahnweiler about his mistress Éva Gouel: "I love her very much and I will write it on my pictures."[9] Éva is the woman referred to by the words "Ma Jolie" that can be seen in many of his Cubist works. When he met Marie-Thérèse Walter in January 1927, his marital situation obliged him to keep this new love-affair a secret, but he revealed it in coded fashion, in a way that could be understood only by those who knew about it. Painting the young woman's portrait outright would have been too risky, so he drew her initials—"MT"[10]—in such a way that they take on an erotic significance: the vertical line of the "T" intersects the "legs" of the "M", on the "bed" formed by the body of the guitar.[11] The object represented is indeed a guitar, hanging by its strap from a nail in the wall. Here we see the persistence of Cubism: the guitar is often represented in Cubist compositions, where the analogy with the female form is easy enough to see. The pictorial vocabulary also derives from Cubism: just a few lines—nail, strap, strings—suffice to give meaning to the white space in the middle of the painting, cut out like a *papier collé*; similarly, a vaguely sketched moulding indicates the wall.

Guitar, 1927, private collection

35 *Guitar*, 27 April 1927, Paris. Oil and charcoal on canvas, 81 x 81 cm

The Bathers

36-39

Picasso spent the summers of 1928 and 1929 at Dinard and painted a series of small canvases representing bathers on the beach. "These pictures are full of symbols like keys, locks, and beach-cabins, empty or transparent, closed or being closed. They are very poetic in inspiration, and were much appreciated by the Surrealists."[1] The prosaic theme of the beach-cabin, which appeared for the first time in the Cannes sketchbook of 1927 and lasted until 1938, the metamorphoses to which Picasso subjects the female anatomy, the combination of the familiar and the monstrous, of humour and mystery as well as the latent eroticism of these little beach scenes, are fully in keeping with the Surrealist aesthetic.

The beach-cabin, both a childhood memory of La Coruña and a concrete motif from the seaside resorts, is a symbol that gives rise to a number of interpretations. Always represented in connection with a bather, this visual metaphor can be said to represent Picasso himself, the house being a symbol of the body, of the inner life, the constantly threatened refuge of inwardness, and beyond that, a place full of mystery. This is why the various women in his life—Olga, Marie-Thérèse, Dora Maar—vainly strive to gain access to it with a key. The key is therefore not only an evident sexual symbol, but also the key of revelation, the key to a hidden significance, to an invisible world. As always in Picasso's work, these little scenes have a double meaning: the starting point is a representation of everyday reality, the living spectacle before the painter's eyes, as we can see in the *Bather with a Ball*, which was inspired by a photograph of Marie-Thérèse, or in the pictures depicting the frantic movements of ball-players in their striped swimsuits. But they are also "magic pictures",[2] mystical contemplations, projections of Picasso's relationship with women and the threat

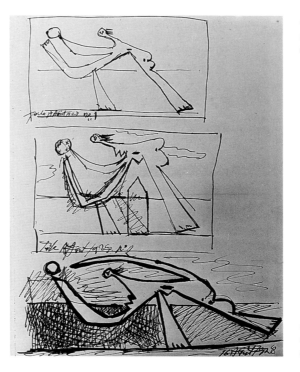

Page from a sketchbook, 1928, private collection

Page from a sketchbook, 1928, private collection

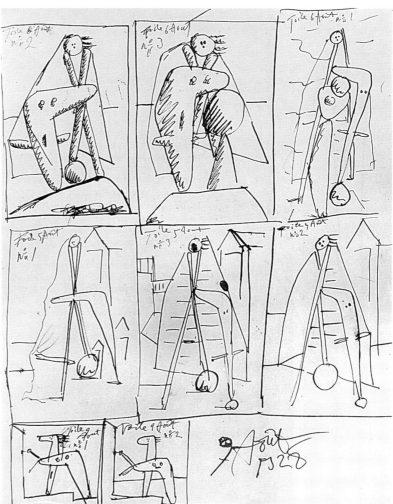

Bather with a Ball, 1929, Musée Picasso, Paris

Marie-Thérèse Walter, 1928, photograph by Picasso, Picasso Archives

they represent for him. At times, the cabin has the appearance of a temple or a tomb, and can even take on the form of the human body, as in the *Large Bather* from 1929 (Musée Picasso, Paris). "Out of a beach cabin Picasso creates a supernatural apparition. Mystery lies within. . . . A reminder of reality, a human form casts its shadow on the sunlit door."[3]

If at the beginning of the twenties the beach was the setting for antique idylls, after the Cannes sketchbook it becomes the backdrop for the elaboration of imaginary sculptures, a stage for the monstrous. In this fantastic imagery the female body has been deformed, dislocated, and reconstructed from bits and pieces; a new anatomical alphabet has been devised, an organic grammar that will be the matrix of all the forms to come. The transparent light of the northern beaches, the bright colours applied in impasto, the brisk, plastic brushstrokes, all accentuate the vital lyricism of the series and contribute to the joyful and poetic atmosphere.

36 *Ball-Players on the Beach*, 15 August 1928, Dinard. Oil on canvas, 24 x 34.9 cm

37 *Bathers*, 6 August 1928,
Dinard. Oil on canvas, 22 x 14 cm

38 *Bather Unlocking a Cabin*, 9 August 1928,
Dinard. Oil on canvas, 32.8 x 22 cm ▷

39 *Bather on the Beach*, 12 August 1928, Dinard. Oil on canvas, 21.5 x 40.4 cm

40 The Swimmer
La nageuse

Although painted in Paris, this female swimmer belongs to the series of "Bathers" that Picasso executed at Dinard in the summers of 1928 and 1929. She moves through the water—or is she floating in mid-air?—her body completely dislocated and malleable, yet still graceful. The head has mutated into a hand (the interchanging of head and hand, usually a tiny head and an enormous hand, is often found in the artist's work); the nose has become the index-finger, and the profile is continued by the knuckle. To occupy as much of the pictorial space as possible and fit into the shape of the canvas, the body has been elongated and deformed to such a degree that the picture can be viewed any way up. This bather-cum-siren seems to be the materialization of one of Picasso's childhood nightmares: he had a recurrent and frightening dream in which his arms and legs became enormous, then fell apart in all directions, while other people around him were undergoing the same transformation. The body that pivots around a central point, deformed and grotesque, recurs in his "Acrobats" series. "It would be a mistake to suspect [Picasso] of painting monstrosities for their own sake . . . . The figures represented appear to be quite well 'put together' and entirely plausible. The artist has been quite arbitrary in determining their structures and proportions, and while these creatures may appear to belong to a Cyclopean realm, they are nonetheless natural, and all the more poignant and beautiful for attaining such a degree of truth."[4]

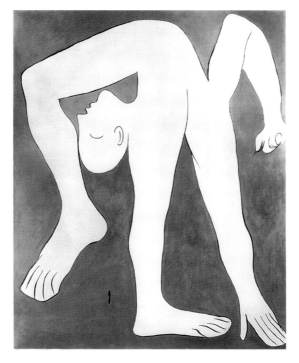

The Blue Acrobat, 1929, Musée National d'Art Moderne, Paris

The Acrobat, 1930, Musée Picasso, Paris

40 *The Swimmer*, November 1929, Paris. Oil on canvas, 130 x 162 cm

41 Figure
Figure

A statue made of "nothing", of "void": that is what, in Apollinaire's story[5], the painter (Picasso) must execute in honour of his friend, the poet Croniamental. The prophetic description applies perfectly to the projects for a monument to Apollinaire that Picasso designed in 1928.

Metal wire appears for the first time in Picasso's work in his sets for the ballet *Mercury* in 1924, which are related to the abstract style of the sketchbook from Juan-les-Pins (Musée Picasso, Paris). In the ballet sets curvilinear graphic forms predominate, while in the drawings the forms are defined by lines and dots. Later, in sketches done at Dinard in 1928, Picasso drew figures constructed solely from straight lines. These sketches were his designs for the Apollinaire monument.

The three original models that were made from iron rods with the help of Julio González are today in the Picasso Museum. Two full-size versions were later constructed; one is in The Museum of Modern Art in New York, the other in the garden of the Picasso Museum.

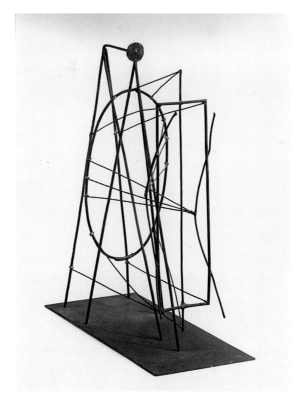

Figure, 1928, Musée Picasso, Paris

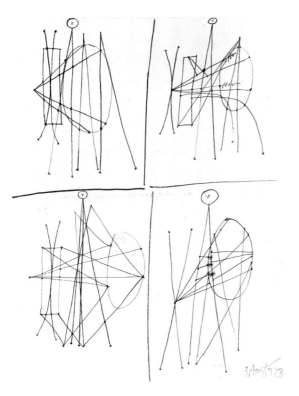

These openwork sculptures are the projection into space of a linear and geometric style of drawing that may also be seen in paintings from this period, for example, *The Studio* from 1928 (The Museum of Modern Art, New York). The construction of the present figure, best seen from the side, involves a succession of four vertical planes connected by oblique lines. The larger rectangle contains the disk-shaped head and the triangle of the upper body. Another rectangle through which all of the oblique lines pass seems to represent the abdomen. In front, the arms are rendered by two curved elements tipped by tiny forged hands and connected to the rest of the sculpture by four lines converging in one point. At the back, a triangle welded to an arc anchors the obliques. The rods correspond to lines of force that animate and subtend the space. This spatialization concept was one of the most revolutionary and fruitful developments in contemporary sculpture, and was later exploited by others, Calder in particular. Yet, for all the technical and formal innovations, Picasso preserves the human form and treats the figure with irony and tenderness.

◁ *Page from a sketchbook*, 1928, private collection

41 *Figure*, autumn 1928, Paris. Iron rods and sheet metal, 60.5 x 15 x 34 cm ▷

On the Fringes od Surrealism II

42 Large Nude in a Red Armchair
Grand nu au fauteuil rouge

To "wound" the viewer, Picasso did not need to
stick razor-blades around his pictures, as he once
thought of doing.[1] There are paintings of his in
which the cruelty is above all artistic, and they can
hurt every bit as surely by their sheer pictorial
power. The *Large Nude in a Red Armchair* is
among these painful visions that make us resonate
with our innermost suffering, the concrete expression of which is complete bodily collapse and a
mute cry of anguish. Everything in the picture con-
tributes to this idea: the elongated limbs, drooping
like "pendant viscera"[2] with stumps instead of
hands and feet, limply draped over the armchair
like the tentacles of an octopus (a sculptural equi-
valent of this flaccid figure may be seen in a contemporary *Seated Woman* in the Picasso
Museum), the head reduced to a toothy maw
whose vice-like form also appears in *The Crucifixion* (pl. 44), the body shrivelled up and emptied of
its substance, and the strident reds, purples and
yellows that stand out against the black outlines.
The pictorial tension of the composition is reinforced by the contrast between the limpness and
elasticity of the body and armchair and the strong

*Page from a sketch-
book*, 1929, Musée
Picasso, Paris

Woman in an Armchair, 1927, Musée Picasso, Paris

Seated Woman,
1929, Musée
Picasso, Paris

42 *Large Nude in a Red Armchair*, 1929, Paris. Oil on canvas, 195 × 129 cm ▷

geometrical architecture that encloses the figure on all sides.

"No matter how horrible or hideous the thing suggested, painting is still what prevails."[3] We can see in earlier sketches that also show a woman in an armchair, and in the anatomical deformations elaborated in the Dinard "Bathers", how Picasso came to this expressive violence, in which he fully reveals his aggressivity toward women.

"No painter has ever loved, hated and feared women so deeply. None has ever been so obsessed by them and bent on their destruction."[4] The poet Paul Éluard remarked upon seeing the analysis of Picasso's handwriting that was published in *Le Point* in 1952: "He loves with intensity, and he kills what he loves."

The years from 1927 to 1929 were dominated by this disquieting and enigmatic vision, in which women often appear as grotesque and menacing monsters. The motif of the picture/mirror—here represented opaque and empty—appears in other works from the period, in some cases reflecting the silhouette of the painter's profile, in others the face of a monstrous woman. These images are probably allusions to his marital difficulties with Olga.

43   The Woman in the Garden
La femme au jardin

This sculpture of iron bars and plates, one of Picasso's most monumental, was the product of his collaboration with Julio González. The two artists had already known each other for a long time, but in 1928, feeling the need to return to sculpture, Picasso worked regularly in González's Montparnasse studio, where he could benefit from his compatriot's tools and know-how. This collaboration resulted in a number of sculptures: three heads, including a *Woman's Head* on the same lines as that of *The Woman in the Garden*, and a black-and-white *Head* of which there is also a painting, and the three scale models of the monument to Apollinaire (pl. 41). Elements found in paintings from this period are easily identifiable: the large fig-leaves (also represented in a 1931 canvas, *The Lamp*[5]), the triangular head with toothy mouth and windswept hair, derived from paintings from 1928/

Head, 1928, Musée Picasso, Paris

Female Head, 1929/30, Musée Picasso, Paris

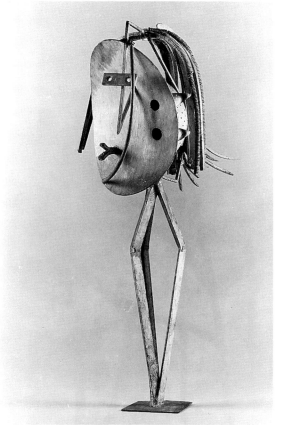

43   *The Woman in the Garden*, 1929, Paris. Welded and painted iron, 206 x 117 x 85 cm   ▷

29. The bean-shaped element and the disk with the hole are anatomical indications for the stomach and sex. Picasso here associates the woman with plant forms to stress the idea of fertility, and this is one of the persistent features of his later portrayals of Marie-Thérèse. In this sculpture, however, neither the shape of the head, nor the skeletal body, nor the aggressively humorous, grinning expression suggest his young mistress. The figure is closer to the harpies and monsters of the paintings from the late twenties.

As in his Cubist constructions and in the wire models, Picasso integrates empty space and hollow volume as compositional elements. He fills out the rigid and abstract metallic structure with realistic details cut out of sheet metal. The combination of two sculptural idioms—the plane and the line in space—is characteristic of Picasso's sculpture from the period 1928-32. The assemblage of different elements is unified by the coat of white paint.

González executed a second, bronze version of this unusual sculpture, which gravitates between abstraction and figuration, half-Constructivist and half-Surrealist. The two works were exhibited at the Georges Petit gallery in Paris in 1932, and inspired André Breton to the comment: "Between these indisputably twin statues there was an exchange of all the considerations of a slightly ironic philosophy, considerations that are necessary when one begins to touch on the question of fate."[6]

44 The Crucifixion
La Crucifixion

The religious subject, the complexity of the formal vocabulary, and the particularly strident colour-scheme of this picture make it one of Picasso's outstanding works. Painted between *The Dance* (1925, Tate Gallery, London) and *Guernica* (1937, Prado Museum, Madrid), it is among the landmark pictures that summarize the artist's aesthetic world, and that have inspired very diverse interpretations.

Given his desire to renew pictorial tradition, it was only to be expected that Picasso would one day be confronted with this major theme of Western painting. He came to choose a Christian sub-

ject not only because of his Spanish roots, but also because of the anticlerical and sacrilegious stance of Surrealism, and because of the place given to medieval iconography at the time in the art journals *Cahiers d'Art* and *Documents*. Beyond its obvious universal symbolism, the theme allowed Picasso to express in metaphorical form his personal preoccupations. He was one of the few artists in the twentieth century of sufficient stature to tackle the history-painting, and in his hands it took on another dimension: in works like *Guernica* and *The Crucifixion*, Picasso charged the event with new significance by incorporating into it his private universe.

Some of the motifs are easily identifiable: Christ on the cross, the two minute empty crosses—one on the right against a red background, the other at bottom left against blue—the bodies of the two thieves at bottom left, the centurion-cum-picador with the spear, the figure at the top of the ladder driving nails into Christ's hands, and the soldiers throwing dice on a drum for his tunic. To these traditional motifs of the crucifixion Picasso has added and freely interpreted a number of other figures. Earlier and later drawings permit us to understand the evolution of these forms and their meaning. Picasso took different elements from previous compositions and put them together like a puzzle, hence the complexity of this work, which is a veritable glossary of his pictorial vocabulary of the pre-

Page from a sketchbook, 1930, artist's estate

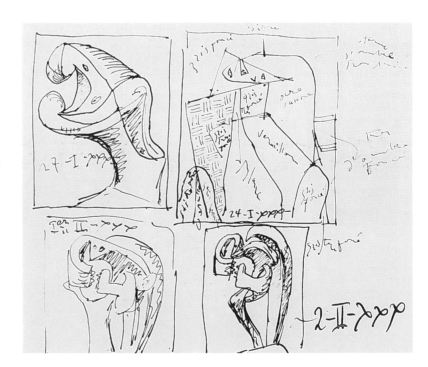

44   *The Crucifixion*, 7 February 1930, Paris. Oil on plywood, 51.5 x 66.5 cm vious five years. The cartilaginous blue head with mantis-like jaws may be seen in the *Seated Bather* (The Museum of Modern Art, New York) and in a sketch dated February 1930. The yellow arms and hands clasped heavenward belong to the figure of Mary Magdalen; her head with the prominent nose is pitched forward and merges with the head of a soldier. The ecstatic pose of Mary Magdalen in supplication was studied very precisely in drawings from 1929; in these sketches, Picasso pushes the contortion of the body to the extreme, so that the face coincides with the small of the back, thus accentuating the phallic character of the breasts and nose. This head/buttocks fusion is illustrated by the red and yellow figure, like a sun with hair, which could also be interpreted as the head of Saint John. Its formal counterpart is the green blob on the left, which some have interpreted as the sponge soaked in vinegar and others as a huge boulder falling from the sky to crush the bird and the figure with the monumental head. This last head is derived from a 1930 sketchbook and can be seen in other pictures. The white figure in the middle, pressed against the body of Christ, is Mary; it presents the same tooth-filled mouth as the *Large Nude in a Red Armchair* (pl. 42) and the flat legs of *The Acrobat* from 1930 (Musée Picasso, Paris). The moon-like face shown frontally and in profile on a yellow triangle to the right of Christ represents Marie-Thérèse; she is seen in this form in a painting from November 1929.[7]

Study for "Parade", 1917, Musée Picasso, Paris

Head, 1929, Paloma-Lopez Picasso Collection, New York

◁ *Crucifixion*, 1917, Musée Picasso, Paris

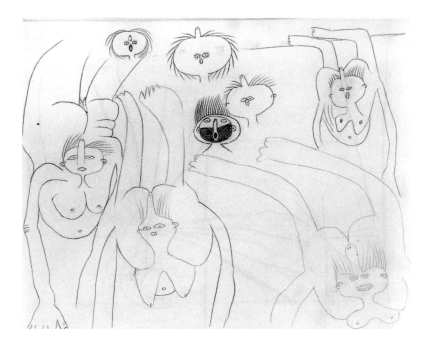

Crucifixion: page from a sketchbook, 1929, Musée Picasso, Paris

Page from a sketchbook, 1930, artist's estate

The picture presents a synthesis both formal—flat, bony and flaccid forms derived from *The Dance* and the Dinard "metamorphoses"—and iconographical. When we look at earlier drawings of *The Crucifixion* (from 1927 and 1929), we see that Picasso combines this theme with other sources: the corrida—evoked by the picador-like figure—and the theatre. An identical ladder is represented on the stage-curtain of *Parade* and in the drawing of 1930 that shows a figure climbing toward the sun. *The Crucifixion* from 1917, which is close to the sketches for *Parade*, already presents the two crosses, the centurion on horseback and the figure of Mary Magdalen in supplication at Christ's feet. As Ruth Kaufmann[8] and Roland Penrose rightly observe, the crucifixion is interpreted here as a ritual sacrifice not unlike the Mithraic cult with its sacrificial bull and solar symbolism.

This last theme is also mentioned by Georges Bataille in an important text published in *Documents* in 1930, *Soleil pourri* ("Rotten Sun"). The moon/sun duality, illustrated by the double face on the right, is also implicit in the two spherical forms on either side of the Christ figure. The boulder or sponge-like form could therefore be interpreted as the "rotten sun" and the red and yellow crescent as the moon, in opposition to the radiant solar sphere on the right. A 1930 drawing[9] shows the traditional crucifixion motifs of the sun and the moon.

Picasso represents the crucifixion in its most savage and brutal aspect, as a primitive ritual sacrifice. The colour-scheme echoes this vision: the blood red and radiant yellow in opposition to the livid bodies of Mary and Christ and the darkness that fell upon the earth at his death. The dissonant hues and the contorted figures with dislocated and intermingled limbs fully render the violence of an apocalyptic cataclysm.

45 *Standing Bather*, 14 August 1930, Juan-les-Pins.
Sand on the back of a stretched canvas, objects,
cardboard and plant-matter sewn and glued on the
canvas, 33 x 24.5 x 2 cm

46 *Face with Two Profiles*, 14 August 1930, Juan-les-Pins.
Sand on the back of a stretched canvas, cardboard sewn
and glued on the canvas. 41 x 33 x 1.5 cm

47 *Object with Palm-Frond*, 27 August 1930, Juan-les-Pins.
Sand on the back of a stretched canvas,
plant-matter, cardboard, nails and objects glued
and sewn on the canvas, 25 x 33 x 4.5 cm

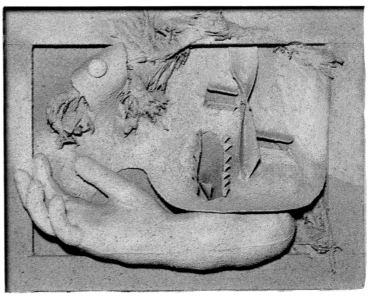

48 *Composition with Glove*, August 1930, Juan-les-Pins.
Sand on the back of a stretched canvas,
glove, cloth, objects, cardboard and plant-matter sewn
and glued on the canvas, 27.5 x 35.5 x 8 cm ▷

49 *Composition with Butterfly*, 1932, Boisgeloup. Cloth, wood, plants, string, thumbtack, butterfly, oil on canvas, 16 x 22 x 2.5 cm

45-48 Reliefs with Sand

These poetic little *tableaux-reliefs*, Surrealistic objects par excellence, form a complete and unique series in Picasso's work. They were made in the summer of 1930 at Juan-les-Pins, and both material—sand and objects found on the beach by the treasure-hunting artist—and subject-matter—bathers and beach life—attest to their origin. Picasso is known to have been very fond of collecting found objects and odds and ends, which he used in his works throughout his career: in the Cubist constructions of 1912-15, the collages of 1926, the assemblages of 1938. He chose these objects not only for their formal suggestivity, their potential for metamorphosis, but also for their poetic impact, their hidden meanings, and he put them together in unexpected combinations. Here, the objects are the usual bric-à-brac of the beachcomber—twigs, bits of string and cloth, rubber ball, seaweed, palm-fronds, toy boat—along with pieces of felt. Picasso sewed or glued them onto the back of the canvas, such that the stretcher serves as a makeshift frame, and then coated them with sand to give them a homogeneous appearance and mask the differences in materials.

Picasso had used sand before: during the Cubist period in some paintings and sculptures, then in a number of paintings in 1924. It is in these little works, however, that it takes on its full meaning, both materially and symbolically. It gives the picture a crisp, grainy roughness that immediately brings the beach and its pastimes to mind. Yet, like the coat of ash and lava that covered the bodies at Pompeii, it also evokes a protective veil that covers living objects and immobilizes them forever. These "picture-reliefs" are like a materialization of the mysterious process of dreaming, in which strange buried images emerge from the unconscious. This impression of a "revealed mystery" is heightened by the fact that the objects are placed on the back of the canvas, as if they showed what was hidden behing the picture. "The hand that appears in the sand-painting is like the upwelling of the unconscious in the midst of everyday objects."[10]

Neither painting nor sculpture, but somewhere in between, these are the works in which Picasso captures to the "highest degree a spirit, not of contradiction, but of escape".[11] They are prime poetic examples of the "privilege of whimsicality" which is accorded the great.[12]

49 Composition with Butterfly
Composition au papillon

A thumbtack, some matchsticks, a piece of cloth, a bit of string, a linden leaf and a butterfly, glued on a canvas, are covered with a coat of creamy white paint, except for the delicate, dappled wings of the butterfly and the fine lacework of the leaf, the only signs of life in this artistic composition. Using familiar, yet startling, objects, Picasso created the little masterpiece that so impressed André Breton, a poetic work in which the marvellous is caught as if by magic in the net of reality.

On the left is a figure with a thumbtack head, matchstick arms and legs, and a piece of cloth for a body; on the right is another figure, formed by frayed pieces of string; between them are an element from the plant world, a leaf chosen both for its delicate texture and for its symbolic significance, and a real butterfly gently resting on the canvas, with a train of brush-hairs caught in the paint. "It was in 1932", writes André Breton, "that for the first time an actual butterfly took its place in a pictorial composition, and it did so without making everything around it immediately turn to dust, and without jeopardizing in any way by its presence, and the overwhelming images that it could inspire, the system of human representations in which it was included."[13]

Twenty years after introducing the piece of oil-cloth into the *Still-Life with Wickerwork Chair* (pl. 14), Picasso repeated the radical gesture of incorporating a "foreign body"—here an insect— into a pictorial mode of representation. The subtle passage from the animate to the inanimate, from the material world to the dream world, from objects to the plant and animal realms, is a perfect illustration of Picasso's artistic genius. For him, art and life were closely linked, and anything could be turned into a painting. The harmonization of these so very different elements is effected by the opaque white paint, which plunges them into an unreal, milky atmosphere. The whole picture is illuminated by the unexpected presence of the butterfly, which takes on a new life in this context.

50-52 Wooden Sculptures

These small wooden sculptures are a further demonstration of Picasso's inventive genius and of his ability to create figures out of whatever objects he happened to have at hand. The elongated forms—carved directly out of pine or lindenwood at Boisgeloup, where he returned to sculpture—may be seen as prefigurations of Giacometti, and they also point to primitive, archaic sources.

It has often been said—and rightly so—that Picasso's sculptures arose from his painting and that there was an interplay between the two media throughout his career. While much has been made of his assemblages of scrap objects, his sculptures in the true sense of the word—that is, involving direct work on resistant materials and the discovery of forms emerging as the block is carved—have

Seated Woman, 1930, Musée Picasso, Paris

Standing Woman, 1930, Musée Picasso, Paris

received much less attention. These figures, which are perfect examples of this aspect of his activity, refer back to the primitivist works of 1907 inspired by Gauguin and Oceanic art. Picasso's stylistic concerns in 1930, however, were of a different order: the forms, which are softer and more refined, derive from the metamorphoses of 1927/28, which introduced whole new possibilities of anatomical transformation.

In the *Couple*, a small-scale masterpiece that recalls Brancusi's famous *Kiss*, the figures are so fused in their embrace that the heads merge and the limbs are practically indistinguishable from the block of wood. In the enigmatic *Female Bust* (pl. 51) with prominent nose, the artist has followed the grain of the wood to create a curvilinear rhythm; the "blank" modelling of the face is similar to that in the heads of Marie-Thérèse from 1931 ff. (pl. 57). More majestic and disquieting is the tall figure of the *Standing Woman* (pl. 52), with head half hollowed out and a body scored with deep incisions; she stands as if balanced on a ball like a clown, with one arm higher than the other. A piece of wire is wound around the neck to hold the arm in place, and perhaps also to suggest a necklace. These small, yet monumental, statuettes also exist in bronze versions.

50 *Couple*, 1930, Boisgeloup. Sculpted lindenwood, 10.5 x 3.5 x 2.2 cm

Standing Woman, 1930, Musée Picasso, Paris

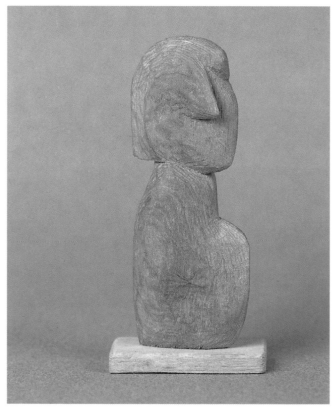

51 *Female Bust*, 1930, Boisgeloup. Sculpted pine, 13 x 5 x 2.5 cm

52 *Standing Woman*, 1930, Boisgeloup. Sculpted pine and wire, 47.5 x 5 x 7.5 cm

53 Figures on the Seashore
Figures au bord de la mer

Frozen in their monstrous embrace like petrified bones, these monumental *Figures on the Seashore* plunge us deeply into Picasso's world of fantasy and eroticism, while the imagery and symbolism show his affinity with Surrealism. Their sheer suggestive power aside, they are a masterful demonstration of Picasso's invention and elaboration of a new formal and pictorial vocabulary.

With its warm, golden light, seaside decor with beach-cabin, and ochre, beige and pink colourscheme, the picture belongs to the "Bathers" series, as does the contemporary *Woman Throwing a Stone* (pl. 54). The theme is related to that of the 1920 pictures, and the forms more specifically to those elaborated at Cannes (1927) and Dinard (1928/29, pl. 36-39). Picasso's "metamorphoses" of the female anatomy were inaugurated in *The Dance* of 1925 (Tate Gallery, London), found a first culmination in the Cannes and Dinard "Bathers", and were reassessed in *The Crucifixion* of 1930 (pl. 44). The formal evolution continued in the *Seated Bather* of 1930 (The Museum of Modern Art, New York), the two 1931 "Bathers", and the paintings and sculptures of the Boisgeloup period (heads of Marie-Thérèse, pl. 57; *Woman in a Red Armchair*, pl. 58), which display the same treatment of body and face as abstract, organic, bone-like forms. These formal innovations may also be compared to the studies for the 1932 *Crucifixion* after Grünewald (Musée Picasso, Paris), in which the human body is reduced to a skeletal form. There is nothing morbid about these figures, however; they are far removed from Tanguy's bony madrepores and Dali's limp and drooping forms. They should be considered more specifically in the light of their relationship to the sculpture of this period.

The sexual metaphors are explicit enough: faces reduced to large mouths reminiscent of the nightmarish *vagina dentata*, sharp tongues thrusting like knives, phallic noses, oversize penis, deformed limbs. The forms interpenetrate and clash in a stony and cruel embrace, like a surreal technical model. The man is indistinguishable from the woman, so intertwined are their attributes. The organic forms—breasts, thighs, legs—are still identifiable, but reduced to smooth and pure rounded monoliths that make the human body appear like a sculpted monument.

The sexual aggressivity and brutality displayed in the female nudes of this period are not solely the product of Picasso's imagination or projections on woman, but also expressions of a reality, namely, the transformations and metamorphoses of the body during the sexual embrace. All of the images and signs refer to concrete and subjective sensations, which are translated into visible form by the artist's pictorial genius. They are perfect illustrations of what André Breton called the "inner model". But Picasso diverges from the other Surrealist painters in that he refuses to abandon the world of perceivable appearance, striving rather to express it with a maximum economy of signs. "Picasso's Surrealism is not the encounter between the real and the imaginary, but the clash of two different realities, both perceptual: pictorial reality and the reality of things."[14]

In the words of Pierre Reverdy: "The image is a creation of the mind. It cannot arise from a comparison, but from the connection between two more or less distanced realities. The more distant and apposite the relations between the two realities, the more powerful the image will be."[15]

This distance, and the shock of the encounter, results in the complete discombobulation of the image.

The beach-cabin, a symbol introduced in the Dinard pictures, appears as an ironic reminder of the civilized world, which contrasts with the savage and primitive instincts of these prehistoric monsters.

54 Woman Throwing a Stone
Femme lançant une pierre

In this picture Picasso takes simplification and abstraction—and therefore painting *per se*—even further. The forms have become difficult to identify: the breasts and triangular belly are recognizable enough, even though there are no realistic indications, but it is hard to make out the head, which has become a sort of phallic shape with antennae, and the arms and legs present even more of a puzzle. A preparatory drawing in one of the sketchbooks shows that the head was more pronounced in its original form.

The mineral character of the body is accentuated by the presence of the boulder and the stone, with which it merges. The monolithic forms assembled in a wonderfully precarious equilibrium make of the female body something like a dolmen, and the huge arm holding the stone gives the construction the appearance of a catapult. Gone are the sunny naturalistic settings of previous years, the beach and sea having given way to an abstract, greyish-white space whose texture has a strong pictorial presence. Only the title remains as a reference to conventional reality.

This stark picture, which is related to the "Bathers" from Dinard (pl. 36-39) and the Boisgeloup heads (pl. 57), contains a wealth of pictorial and suggestive possibilities: the arabesques of the rock counterbalanced by those of the body, the convoluted form, the suppleness of the volumes, the pinkish and stony-grey colours. The figure and its space

Page from a sketchbook, 1931, artist's estate

53   *Figures on the Seashore*, 12 January 1931, Paris. Oil on canvas, 130 x 195 cm

54   *Woman Throwing a Stone*, 8 March 1931, Paris. Oil on canvas, 130.5 x 195.5 cm

have been rendered ambiguous solely by painterly means, and the result is as disturbing to the eye as it is to the tactile sense. Picasso here announces the bold and sketchy manner of the 1970s: rich impasto, plastic paintwork, drippings, and visible brushwork.

plays on the morphological ambiguities of limbs; for example, the top of the left arm can be read as another figure. The book has also been treated in a peculiar manner; it has taken on the form of a wedge-shaped stone block, and the lines of writing look almost like the impression of a thumbprint.

55 Large Bather with a Book
Grande baigneuse au livre

The theme of the nude bather on the beach has returned once again, but the full and smooth forms of 1931 have hardened and become more geometric, and the combination of faceted masses and hollows recalls the Cubist style. With the alternation of sharp-edged and rounded forms, this body is more like an architecture than a human figure; one can easily imagine air circulating between these arms as solid as pillars.

The pose of the figure, leaning forward and forming an oval, will be repeated in another figure many years later: the woman bathing her feet in Picasso's version of Manet's *Luncheon on the Grass* (*Le Déjeuner sur l'herbe*, 1960/61, pl. 96). The way the body closes in on itself may be explained by the reading position, but it also corresponds to the logic inherent in this type of construction based on volumes.

With this painting, which shows affinities with the contemporary *Bathing-Scene* (Guggenheim Museum, New York), Picasso begins a new phase in his "Bathers" series. The erotic element has disappeared and given way to more intimate scenes that are full of humour, fantasy and mystery. The monstrous element is not far away, though, as we can see in another work from the same year, *Two Nude Women on the Beach* (Musée Picasso, Paris), which recalls the pictorial fantasmagorias of the Dinard period. The two canvases were not painted during a seaside sojourn, but in Picasso's new studio at Le Tremblay-sur-Mauldre or in Paris, in the Rue des Grands-Augustins. The uniform and neutral seaside decor serves to set off the three-dimensional quality of the figures.

The colours—pink, grey and blue—streaked with white, and the use of pastel powder, give the body a coarse and friable appearance. Picasso

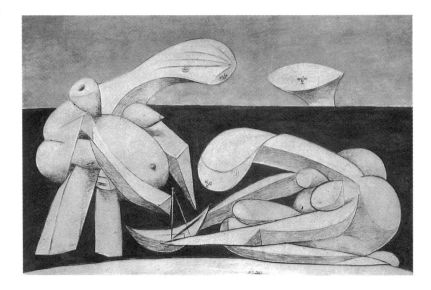

Bathing-Scene, 1937, Peggy Guggenheim Collection, Venice

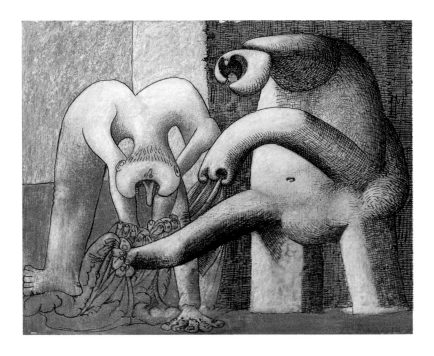

Two Nude Women on the Beach, 1937, Musée Picasso, Paris

55 *Large Bather with a Book*, 18 February 1937, Paris. Oil, pastel and charcoal on canvas, 130 × 97.5 cm

Boisgeloup and Marie-Thérèse

56   Large Still-Life with Pedestal Table
Grande nature morte au quéridon

Few still-lifes in Picasso's work achieve such monumentality and such a colourful exuberance as this
one, which contains fairly transparent allusions to
his mistress Marie-Thérèse Walter. The generosity
of the curvaceous forms, especially the two green
apples with black dots, the play of arabesques,
and the dominant yellows and purples all belong to
the pictorial vocabulary reserved for representations of Marie-Thérèse, which can be seen in such
works as the *Woman Reading* of 1932 and the *Reclining Nude* (pl. 60).

This particular vocabulary was inspired both by
the characteristics of his mistress's anatomy and by
the artist's return to free-standing sculpture when
he set up his new studio at Boisgeloup. Picasso
includes standard motifs from his still-life repertory:
the tripod table—which may also be seen in
Braque's large still-lifes—the white fruit bowl with
its three fruits, and the large yellow pitcher, whose
forms recall the playful lines of the 1926 *Painter and
His Model* (pl. 34). Everything here seems to be in
motion, twisting, undulating, overflowing with vitality: the table legs, the spirals of the pitcher handle,
and even the lines of the wall and floor. Nothing
arrests the curvilinear energy. The organic, ovoid or
genital, forms of the fruit, bowl and table legs are
symbols of fertility; they correspond well to the artist's vision of Marie-Thérèse as a young woman
about to bloom. And so she is often represented in
association with fruits and plants, as we can see in
other portraits from this period: *Nude in a Garden*
(pl. 61) and *Reclining Nude* (pl. 60). The continuous
black outlines of these three pictures are similar to
those in *The Kiss* (pl. 32) and *The Painter and His
Model* (pl. 34); they enclose the flat and pure colours like the leading of luminous stained-glass windows.

Woman Reading, 1932, Musée Picasso, Paris

56   *Large Still-Life with Pedestal Table*, 11 March 1931, Paris. Oil on canvas, 195 x 130.5 cm   ▷

57 Female Head
Tête de femme

In 1931, in order to escape from his marital problems, Picasso set up a large studio in the newly-purchased Château de Boisgeloup near Gisors. There he devoted himself to free-standing sculpture, inspired by the site and by the presence of an ideal model, Marie-Thérèse, whose image dominates his production in both painting and sculpture during the period from 1931 to 1936.
He executed a number of monumental heads of Marie-Thérèse, ranging from the most classical to the most schematic. Despite his constant anatomical and organic permutations, Picasso always reproduced the particular physical characteristics of his model and the robust fullness of her forms: the almond-shaped eyes, the nose as prolongation of the forehead, the prominent cheekbones, the rounded breasts. The female faces he created are organized into constructions with sexual qualities: the head with phallic nose, the vaginal mouth, the eyes incised into the rounded volumes. This correspondence between facial features and genital organs is a common feature of Neolithic and African art. Picasso himself owned a Nimba fertility mask in which the nose was represented by a protuberance similar to the one seen here. Each organ is treated autonomously, leading eventually to extreme sim-

Nimba Mask, Baga, New Guinea, Musée Picasso, Paris

plification as in the two female heads, reduced here to an assemblage of cylindrical volumes. These sculptures are also depicted in paintings from the same period, as in *The Sculptor* from 1931 (Musée Picasso, Paris).

Studies for "Female Head", 1931, Musée Picasso, Paris

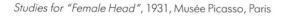

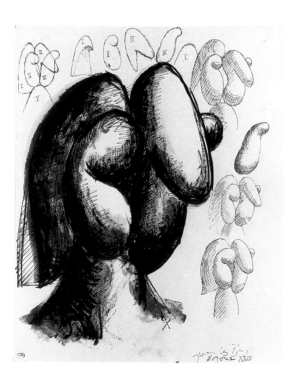

Female Head, 1932, Musée Picasso, Paris

57 *Female Head*, 1931, Boisgeloup.
Plaster, 128.5 x 54.5 x 62.5 cm ▷

58 Woman in a Red Armchair
Femme au fauteuil rouge

The painting of a sculpture, or a painted sculpture? A picture like *Woman in a Red Armchair* reveals the long-standing dialectic between the two modes of expression in Picasso's work. The aspiration toward volume and real space is implicit in the paintings of several periods: in the Cubist epoch, in 1928, and during the Boisgeloup years. Derived from the monolithic forms of the *Figures on the Seashore* (pl. 53), these bone-like elements representing the different parts of a female body anticipate the variations on the crucifixion after Grünewald, in which the human body will be reduced to its final, skeletal state. While the smooth, pinkish limbs of the *Figures on the Seashore* or the Dinard "Bathers" suggest a soft, spongy, fleshy material, the rough bone-shapes in this composition proclaim their mineral hardness and density and their sculptural origins—modelling by light and shade, whitish plaster colouring, interplay of projections and hollows. Sculpture gives painting this feel of surface texture and materiality.

The inclined position of the figure in this work recalls Marie-Thérèse's pose in some contemporary paintings. The round eyes are similar to those of the *Female Head* of 1931 (Musée Picasso,

Woman Seated in a Red Armchair, 1932, Musée Picasso, Paris

Paris). We can recognize the woman's neck, arms, and spherical breasts and belly. Her back merges with that of the chair, which has also been decomposed into separate volumes. The impression of weight, solidity and petrification of the body is counterbalanced by the precarious equilibrium of the construction as a whole. The painting's dramatic aspect, inherent in the morbid representation of the figure, is heightened by the strong chalky light and the contrast between red and black. Picasso's use of bone shapes may be explained by his personal inclinations, the requirements of a particular pictorial logic, and—last but not least—by their macabre symbolism.

The Crucifixion, 1932, Musée Picasso, Paris

58 *Woman in a Red Armchair*, 27 January 1932, Boisgeloup. Oil on canvas, 130.2 × 97 cm ▷

59   Woman with a Stiletto
La femme au stylet

In painting the murder of Marat, the French revolutionary, by Charlotte Corday, Picasso took a
historical theme—underscored by the red, white
and blue flag—to express his own state of mind.
Figures of menacing women had begun to appear
in 1927, at the beginning of his idyll with Marie-
Thérèse. By 1931 his conflicts with his wife Olga
had become unbearable. In this picture she has
evidently been cast as a destructive monster, while
Marat is portrayed with the features of Marie-
Thérèse.

   We are far from David's dignified depiction of
the scene, in which the revolutionary is represented
alone, slumped in his bathtub, still holding his as-
sassin's letter in his hand. The Marat with whom
Picasso seems to be identifying is a flat and sexless
figure with a tiny head and enormous foot, caught
by surprise while he was writing. The scene is like
something out of a horror-film: a shrilly screaming,
predatory woman savagely attacks a frail, de-
fenceless creature. The space seems dense and
close because of the small scale. The woman's
murderous fury magnifies her power, so that she
becomes huge, with tentacular limbs, breasts, hips
and teeth going in all directions. Her limbs seem to
extend endlessly beyond the confines of the room.
She fills the space like a balloon, while her victim
shrinks more and more as his blood flows out and
spreads around him.

   Several works from this period reveal a violent
sexual paranoia, which is expressed either by
pathological aggressivity on the woman's
part—the assassination of Marat is treated in
another work from 1934[1]—or by sexual insatiabil-
ity, as in the *Figures on the Seashore* (pl. 53).

The Murder, 1934, Musée Picasso, Paris

59 *Woman with a Stiletto*, 19–25 December 1931, Paris. Oil on canvas, 46.6 x 61.5 cm

60 Reclining Nude
Nu couché

Picasso's work is traditionally divided into periods defined either in chromatic terms (Blue, Rose) or stylistic terms (Cubist, Neoclassical). To these well-known periods should also be added those in which his art was dominated by a particular woman. For each woman in his life, Picasso developed a specific pictorial vocabulary that corresponded to her general physical characteristics, and to the aesthetical and sentimental feelings she inspired in him. From 1931 to 1936 the figure of Marie-Thérèse Walter, whom he met by chance on the street in 1927 when she was seventeen years old, occupied a prominent place in his painting and sculpture. Although their liaison was kept secret for a long time, Marie-Thérèse was omnipresent in his art. Fate evidently had a hand in their encounter, and Picasso prophetically declared to her when they first met: "We are going to do great things together." His painting from then on became a fantasmagoria of volume and modelling, for Marie-Thérèse's full and vigorous forms were ideally suited to his desire to work on sculpture in the round. She inspired a new vocabulary of line and colour logically derived from the Cannes and Dinard period. Brassaï recalls that "he liked the blondness of her hair, her radiant complexion, her statuesque body. From that day on his painting began to undulate. At no other time in his life was his painting so vibrant, the curves so sinuous, the arms so enveloping, the hair so flowing."[2]

"This *Reclining Nude* belongs to the luxuriant series of sleeping women whose innocent abandon leaves them ripe for erotic delectation."[3]

Highlights with matt white paint are briskly applied like pastel to the body and background to model the forms and to give the picture an extraordinary luminosity. The woman's nudity seems to bathe in a shower of solar particles and bask in a sulphurous warmth. The intensity of the radiant energy is suggested by the brightness of the sun and by the wavy patterns that decorate the wall. The sensual and voluptuous arabesques of the body moulded into a figure-eight are reminiscent of Matisse's *Blue Nude* (1907, Baltimore Museum of Art) and may be seen in a sculpture from the same period *Reclining Bather* (1931, Musée Picasso, Paris).

As in the *Large Still-Life with Pedestal Table* (pl. 56), Picasso associates female sexuality with images of organic, plant-like fertility and ripeness, seen in the pears, the full, fruit-shaped breasts, the large green leaves, and the bean-shaped head enclosed like an embryo in an ovoid space.

Reclining Bather, 1931, Musée Picasso, Paris

60 *Reclining Nude*, 4 April 1932, Boisgeloup. Oil on canvas, 130 x 161.7 cm

61 Nude in a Garden
Nu dans un jardin

In this later nude Picasso takes the transformation of Marie-Thérèse's body a step further, and opens up new possibilities in the painter's art. Everything here seems to be "painted": the brisk and sketchy brushwork, the impasto, the overlayings and transparencies express the painter's exaltation and give the work an extraordinary impression of texture. The passage from a sculptural and linear treatment in the *Reclining Nude* (pl. 60) to a more flexible, dense and entirely pictorial approach is similar to the development that took place between the *Figures on the Seashore* (pl. 53) and the *Woman Throwing a Stone* (pl. 54).

Forms, colours and material unite in a hymn of praise to Marie-Thérèse's body, as if the artist's desire had incarnated itself in paint: the bright pink of the flesh, the luxuriant greenery, the bluish grey of the water, the red and gold of the oriental cushion. The curled-up body has been reduced to an ovoid form; the blond hair in the shape of beanpods, the flowers and plants, and the water are further suggestions of fertility. The black necklace that adorns the long neck defines a jagged, lunar profile on the breast. The supple grace of this female nude is very reminiscent of Matisse.

The image of woman as flower or plant, or as nourishing and fertile ground in which the biological mystery of procreation takes place, has its origins in the most ancient archetypes, and is readily suggested by the body in sleep. Freed from the constraints of consciousness, the "dream body" transforms itself, lends itself to erotic fantasies, and returns to its primitive organic condition. For Picasso, Marie-Thérèse is above all the *sleeping* woman, offered and abandoned to the painter's gaze.

Nude with Bouquet of Irises and Mirror, 1934, Musée Picasso, Paris

61 *Nude in a Garden*, 4 August 1934, Boisgeloup. Oil on canvas, 162 x 130 cm

62 Woman Reading

Femme lisant

The theme of the woman *sleeping*, abandoned in her repose, is followed by that of the woman *reading*, lost in contemplation or meditation. Reading is another form of revery or abstraction from reality, enclosing the woman in a peaceful, silent inner world. It also offers a new pictorial scheme, that of the seated figure with head inclined, resting on the hand, or more or less drooping over the table. The rectilinear table serves as a buttress for the whole composition, which has been simplified to a tight geometric grid. The curvilinear style of Boisgeloup is replaced here by a pattern of sharp, angular forms that trap the figure in a net of triangular shapes, from which only the rounded breasts and head escape (see also the *Nude with Bouquet of Irises and Mirror*, Musée Picasso, Paris). The harmony of yellow and purple and the peculiarly shaped head with prominent nose are characteristic of Picasso's representations of Marie-Thérèse. In the series of women reading, writing or drawing from 1934/35, the hands always have a swallowtail or sheaf-like form. The pointed shape of the book, which looks like a folded paper figure, and the large blue and purple hand bring the fragile image of a bird to mind. The sharpness of the forms is reinforced by the acid tones of yellow, green and purple. This was one of Picasso's most colourful periods, possibly due to the influence of Matisse. The green skirt with tile-like pattern recalls the collages and imitation materials of Cubism and is a prefiguration of the monumental collage representing *Women at Their Toilette* (pl. 73) from 1938, which is entirely composed of pieces of printed wallpaper.

The Muse, 1935, Musée Picasso, Paris

62 *Woman Reading*, 9 January 1935, Paris. Oil on canvas, 162 × 113 cm

63 Woman with Foliage
Femme au feuillage

Like an antique idol, the *Woman with Foliage* stands out as one of the strongest and most mysterious pieces of sculpture of the period. At once prosaic, bizarre and hieratic, it is yet another demonstration of Picasso's genius for metamorphosis, of his ability to transform the humblest materials with a light and poetic touch into figures with a sacred and timeless presence. For this piece, and a number of others, such as *Woman Resting on Her Elbow* (1933, Musée Picasso, Paris), *Bearded Figure* (1933, Musée Picasso, Paris), *Woman with an Orange* (1934), and *The Orator* (1937), the artist used casts of objects and textures to make certain parts of the body, and then modelled the different elements to make a whole. The plaster original was cast in bronze to create a unified form and raise these ordinary materials to a nobler existence. An interesting task for the viever in this type of sculpture is the identification of the original materials. Picasso chose them very deliberately: thus, the corrugated cardboard suggests the folds of archaic drapery, the organic veining of the leaves contrasts with the mechanical pattern of the cardboard, the rectangular matchbox transforms the head into an impenetrable mask. "The heads are square because they should be round."[4] Despite its stiffness, this oracular figure has a striking formal energy. "It seems to be agitated by the fluttering of the leaves, by the rippling folds of the drapery."[5] The association of the human figure with plants is a constant feature of Picasso's art during this period.

Woman with an Orange, 1934, Musée Picasso, Paris

The Orator, 1937, Musée Picasso, Paris

63 *Woman with Foliage*, 1934, Boisgeloup. Bronze, 37.9 x 20 x 25.9 cm ▷

Bullfight and Minotaur

64 Bullfight: Death of the Torero
Corrida: La mort du toréro

A Spaniard in his heart and soul, Picasso was a true *aficionado* and the supreme painter of the bullfight. His oldest memories were of the arena in Málaga where he often went with his father, and his first paintings were devoted to this subject. Each return to Spain was followed by a new series of "Corridas". Everything about the theme appealed to him: not only the dramatic spectacle full of bright and shimmering colours, and the strong contrasts between light and shadow, but also—and especially—the deadly sacrificial combat opposing in ritual confrontation man and animal, horse and bull. For Picasso, the latter duality symbolizes man and woman: the bull stands for the virile strength of the male, while the disembowelled horse represents woman. Between the two a drama is enacted, full of violence, brutality and possession, but also of pleasure and passion. This last aspect is especially apparent in the "Minotaur" series, which is so revelatory of the ambiguity of Picasso's eroticism.

In a swirling mass of flamboyant and exuberant colours dominated by blood-red, bright pink and golden yellow—the traditional colours of the bullfight—the black bull lunges in a headlong charge, tossing up the dead torero and goring the white horse, whose neck twists back in a convulsion of anguish and terror (this figure will reappear in *Guernica*, 1937, Prado Museum, Madrid). The scene is composed in a radial arrangement of flailing extremities, the elliptical figure of the bull framed by the arena forming the hub. The bullfighter is draped over the bull's neck in a position that suggests the abandon and ecstasy of lovemaking, a pose seen in another painting from the same year, *The Death of the Woman Torero*. Here, the scene is depicted close-up, tightly framed, completely filling the pictorial space.

The different handling of the two lateral sections of the picture—the one very detailed and with effects of relief, the other flat and sketchy—accentuates the disequilibrium and the relentless thrust of the animal's charge.

Bullfight: The Death of the Female Torero, 1933, Musée Picasso, Paris

64 *Bullfight: Death of the Torero*, 19 September 1933, Boisgeloup. Oil on wood, 31 x 40 cm

65 Minotaur and Dead Mare in front of a Cave
Minotaure et jument morte devant une grotte

The Minotaur, a creature from ancient Mediterranean mythology, is a key figure in Picasso's imagery. The artist recognized this himself when he said: "If you were to plot on a map all of the places through which I have passed, and then connect the dots with a line, the resulting figure would probably be a Minotaur." The Minotaur is a link between two cultures, relating the bullfight to the Mithraic cult, and the prime symbol of duality. Half man and half beast, it incarnates primitive bestiality, the dark forces of the unconscious, the executioner and his victim, love and death.

The figure of the Minotaur appears for the first time in a large collage from 1928 (Musée National d'Art Moderne, Paris), and reappears in a series of drawings, etchings and gouaches between 1930 and 1937. This crucial and troubled period coincided with the outbreak of the Spanish Civil War and Picasso's surrealistic phase. In his personal life this was a time of severe conflicts in his marriage with Olga, but also of love and eroticism with Marie-Thérèse and Dora Maar.

In the gouache dated 6 May, the Minotaur carries a dead mare in his arms and with his outstretched hand (similar to the one in the famous *Minotauromachy* engraving) pushes away a young girl crowned with flowers who looks at him from behind a veil, seemingly trapped in the grip of a colossal plaster hand. The dark cave on the left from which two hands emerge in a gesture of supplication may be an allusion to the Labyrinth. The Minotaur has a human face and an expression of great sadness: clearly, he represents Picasso himself, and the dead mare, Marie-Thérèse. The young girl with the veil, who is also present in the *Minotauromachy* and some bullfight scenes, represents purity and innocence; she is also an image of Marie-Thérèse. The hands at the mouth of the cave may be interpreted as a reference to Olga—or some other abandoned Ariadne. At the one side, a dark and gaping hole, at the other, daylight: in between, the figure of the Minotaur appears out of nowhere. The evolution in the treatment of the hands, from a diaphanous form to a naturalistic rendition, and finally a plaster hand, gives visible expression to the passage from a nightmarish and chaotic world to the myth of creation, symbolized by the young girl's gaze and the stony hand.

66 Scene from the Minotauromachy: Minotaur's Body in a Harlequin Costume
Scène de la Minotoromachie:
La dépouille du Minotaure en costume d'Arlequin

In the gouache dated 28 May 1936, the Minotaur is dressed in a harlequin costume and is being carried by an eagle-headed monster. This fantastic group of figures, which are of completely opposite natures (the harlequin's hands are feminine, the monster's virile), has as pendant two strange figures: a bearded man (the beard is a traditional attribute of the sculptor) wearing a mare's hide (Marie-Thérèse?) carries an angelic adolescent with flower-adorned hair (Dora Maar?) on his shoulders; this couple is probably an allegory of love. The man threateningly wields a stone. The desolate landscape heightens the tragic mood of the scene.

The artist here represents himself twice: in the figure of Minotaur-Harlequin and as a bearded man in his prime. He is both persecutor and persecuted. These many symbols, which may or may not be related to the artist's life, combine to create an elaborate allegory.

The Minotauromachy, 1935, Musée Picasso, Paris

65 *Minotaur and Dead Mare in front of a Cave*, 6 May 1936, Juan-les-Pins, Gouache and Indian ink, 50 x 65.5 cm ▷

66 *Scene from the Minotauromachy: Minotaur's Body in a Harlequin Costume*, 28 May 1936, Paris. Gouache and Indian ink on paper, 44 x 54.5 cm ▷

Portraits

67 Straw Hat with Blue Foliage
Chapeau de paille au feuillage bleu

Is this a still-life or the portrait of a woman? Picasso here pushes the disarticulation of the human likeness to the extreme. The patch of pink flesh, the semicircular eyes, the twisted nose and mouth, are superimposed on a long purple neck shaped like a vase, which is topped by a hat twisted into a figure-eight and decorated with blue leaves. The neck emerges from a grey and yellow plinth that may be read as a picture-frame. The disorganization of the face—which does not preclude physiognomic familiarity or expressivity—has often been interpreted as an expression of the artist's destructive tendencies and aggressivity toward woman. Picasso treats the body and face as objects that can be disassembled and reassembled at will, according to his own pictorial logic. If the work were completely abstract, without identifiable organic forms, the visual shock would not be so great. The picture succeeds as an expression of provocation, rage, humour, and derision precisely because the incongruous forms preserve human features and expression.

Study for "Straw Hat with Blue Foliage", 1936, Musée Picasso, Paris

67 *Straw Hat with Blue Foliage*, 1 May 1936, Juan-les-Pins. Oil on canvas, 61 x 50 cm

68 Portrait of Dora Maar
Portrait de Dora Maar

A new woman came into Picasso's life in 1936, a young Yugoslavian photographer, Dora Maar, whose real name was Dora Marković. She was a friend of the poet Paul Éluard, frequented Surrealist circles, and spoke Spanish. For several years, portraits of his two "muses"—the blonde Marie-Thérèse and the dark-haired Dora Maar—alternated in Picasso's painting. In this radiant and sumptuously coloured portrait, Dora Maar is represented majestically seated in an armchair, smiling and resting her head on a long-fingered hand. The face is shown in a combined frontal and profile view, with a red eye and a green eye facing in different directions. For many people, these deformations are the very hallmark of Picasso's art. Yet, despite the distortions, or perhaps even because of them, Picasso achieved a striking resemblance that could be said to be "truer than life". The deformations primarily serve an expressive purpose: the idea is less to remake reality than to express its possibilities, to capture all the aspects of the sitter. "Whereas Ingres used the traditional convention of the mirror to represent his model frontally and in profile, as in the portraits of Madame Moitessier and of the Comtesse d'Haussonville, Picasso resorted to a graphic synthesis, a pictorial fusion developed through his Cubist experiments."[1] Every possible pictorial means has been brought into play to "pin down" Dora Maar, to express her physical characteristics, her temperament, and the painter's vision of her. Certain features are specific to this model: the fingernails painted with red polish, the long, graceful hands, the pose, the black hair, the large, dark and staring eyes, the round, wilful chin, and the black, embroidered and laced corsage, which appears in another canvas in the Picasso Museum. The face is given volume by a play of colours and lighting that makes the cheek stand out like a peach. The expression is pleasant but distant; the eyes sparkle with life and intelligence. The pointed forms of the corsage and fingers suggest elegance and distinction. On the other hand, the cross-structures of the chair and of the embroidery, the squared pattern of the skirt, and the vertical and horizontal stripes of the background give the impression of a prison or convent cell, making it seem as if the model were enclosed within the confines of a narrow and cruel mental space.

Portrait of Dora Maar, 1937, Musée Picasso, Paris

68 *Portrait of Dora Maar*, 1937, Paris. Oil on canvas, 92 x 65 cm ▷

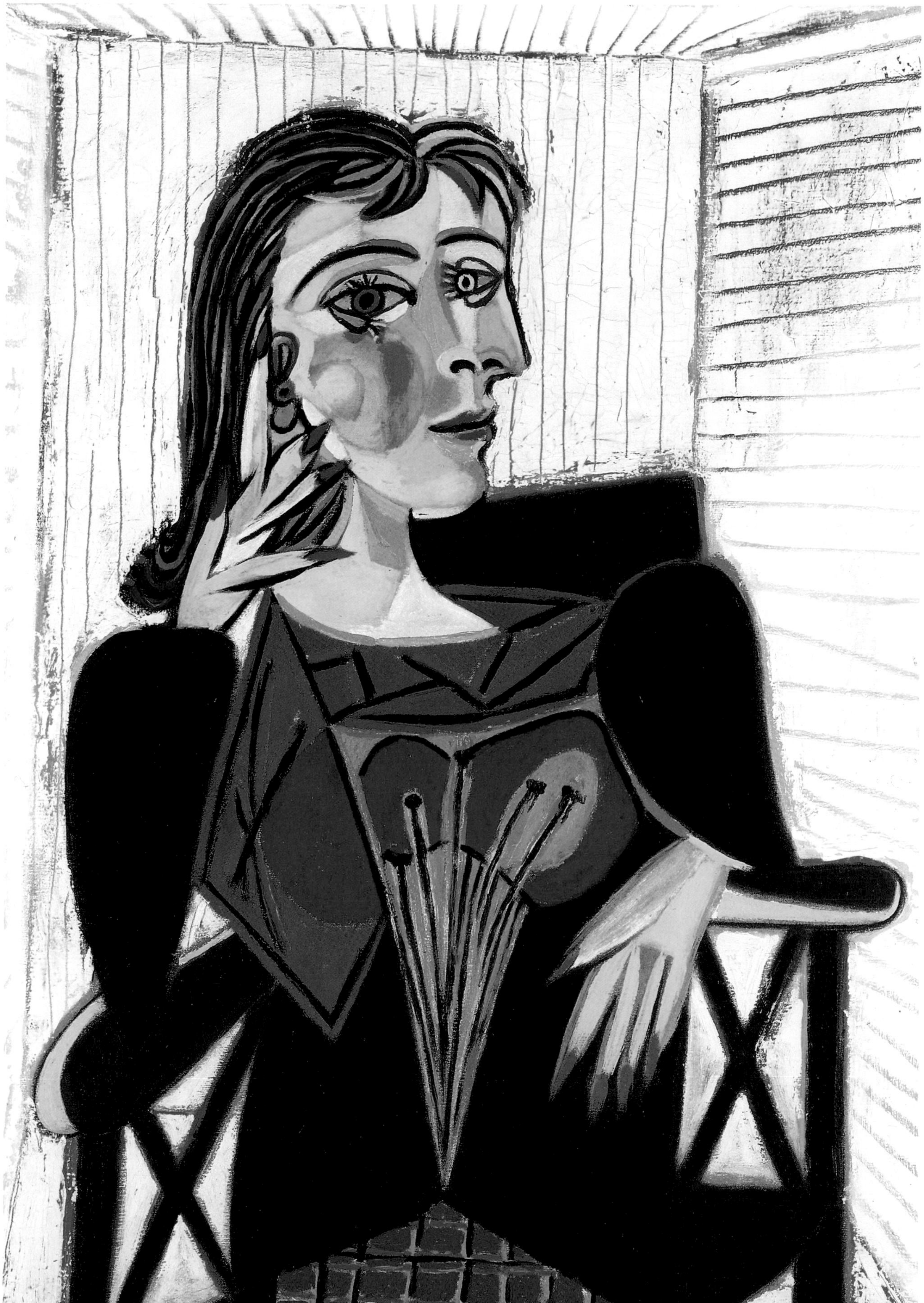

69 Portrait of Marie-Thérèse

Portrait de Marie-Thérèse

While Picasso's pictorial vocabulary for Dora Maar features sharp-edged forms and contrasts of black and red, the forms expressive of Marie-Thérèse retain the characteristics of the Boisgeloup days: decorative arabesques, gently rounded shapes, and soft pastel tones with a dominance of blue and yellow. The body is lithe and supple, the long fingers are like palm-fronds. The face is bathed in cool blues and greens that create a lunar atmosphere of poetic revery and tenderness. The busy striped patterns that look like corrugated cardboard are counterbalanced by the sparing simplicity of the background, which has a box-like appearance owing to the distorted perspective. The long nose that continues the line of the forehead and the pupils overlapping the outline of the eyes like coins are specific features of Marie-Thérèse portraits. The distortion of the face here is more of a pictorial arrangement than a combination of frontal and profile views.

"As regards the portraits of Marie-Thérèse and Dora Maar, it is surprising to note that they are just as much a part of the everyday world of art-reproductions as other well-loved masterpieces—Byzantine icons, classical portraits, the Venuses of Cranach, the regents of Frans Hals, the figures of Velázquez. These two portraits have a powerful presence for us, self-sufficient and expressive of our times."[2]

Portrait of Marie-Thérèse, 1937, Musée Picasso, Paris

69 *Portrait of Marie-Thérèse*, 6 January 1937, Paris. Oil on canvas, 100 x 81 cm

70 Portrait of Nusch Éluard
Portrait de Nusch Éluard

Nusch Benz was Paul Éluard's second wife. They met in 1930 and were married in 1934. Her gentle and fine-featured face inspired Picasso to some very beautiful portraits in quite different styles, which well capture the serenity and radiance of the young woman. In this likeness the artist has succeeded in rendering Nusch's personality in all its subtlety, as well as her elegance, expressed by the clear design of the coat and by the pointed hat decorated with a horseshoe for good luck. The two sides of her character—strength and fragility, like day and night, or life and death—are suggested by the combined lunar and solar face. These oppositions are also represented by the *putti* figures on the lapel bearing a death's head and a torch. The most easily recognizable features are the mouth and the narrow, precisely outlined eyes. Despite such deformations as the double profile and the divergent eyes, Picasso's portraits are always easily identifiable, for he distils the sitter's essential characteristics. The plain background is rare in his portraits of women.

Portrait of Nusch Éluard, 1941, Musée National d'Art Moderne, Paris

71 The Weeping Woman
La femme qui pleure

Considering his interest in representing the full range of human emotions—love, hate, pleasure, pain—it was only natural that Picasso should turn to the theme of the woman in tears. In the autumn of 1937—a dramatic period both in his personal life and in the outer world—he represented this theme obsessively in a variety of mediums: drawing, painting, print, and sculpture. The motif is drawn from *Guernica*, and symbolizes the distress of Spanish women during the Civil War. In these faces he expresses the heartrending conflicts and bitter tribulations of his homeland. At the same time, this type of face alludes to one of the women he loved, Dora Maar, who had an excitable character, and was inclined to "storms and outbursts."[3] The violence of their relationship, documented by the biographers, gives credence to this interpretation, but there were deeper reasons for the association between his mistress and Spain. In Dora Maar, Picasso found a politically active companion who shared his anguish over current events, as well as his artistic concerns. As Pierre Daix notes: "When Picasso imagined the sorrow of the women of his country in 1937, the dark-haired, Spanish-speaking Dora Maar was a more fitting model than the blonde and placid Marie-Thérèse."[4] As in *Guernica*, Picasso blends historical events and his personal life, and in this way achieves a universal significance. Unlike traditional history-painters, he represents horror in the midst of everyday life.

Against a briskly brushed mauve background the woman's dark grey face stands out almost in relief, like something made of earth, the features scratched into the coating of paint. The large, sharp-edged triangle of the handkerchief creates an incongruous and ominous white presence in the middle of the composition, while the yellow-green accents on the nose and hands intensify the feeling of sadness and despair. The face is delineated in simplified and primitive forms: tear-shapes for the eyes, mouth twisted into a grimace of pain, cheek furrowed by tears (these motifs also appear in the studies for the painting). Pierre Daix has estab-

70 *Portrait of Nusch Éluard*, autumn 1937, Paris. Oil on canvas, 92 × 65.2 cm ▷

Page of studies, 1937, Musée Picasso, Paris

The Weeping Woman, 1937, Tate Gallery, London

lished a relationship between the unusual stylistic handling, the strong texturization and the use of black strokes in face and hair, and a visit that Picasso paid Paul Klee around this time. Once again, Picasso demonstrates that he can invent new pictorial means to express new emotions.

The Weeping Woman, 1937, Musée Picasso, Paris

◁ *The Weeper*, 1937, Musée Picasso, Paris

71 *The Weeping Woman*, 18 October 1937, Paris. Oil on canvas, 55.3 x 46.3 cm

72 The Supplicant
La suppliante

Picasso had finished *Guernica* (1937, Prado Museum, Madrid) four months before, but the horrors of the war continued to haunt him. He does not paint war directly, but its presence is implicit in the tragic figures that fill his canvases: women weeping, crying out their anguish, vehemently expressing their grief and suffering. He attacks the forms with a vengeance, so that the expressionistic deformations of the faces and bodies become perfect pictorial equivalents of physical and mental pain. This woman raises her hands heavenward in supplication, giving vent to her protest with every part of her being: the face with its horselike nostrils, tear-shaped eyes, and chin contorted by the scream, the head crowned with a purple veil (the colour of martyrdom), the neck stretched out so thin that it does not seem capable of supporting so large a head, the clothes weighing her down to the ground, the two enormous arms, and the pendant breast with a nipple as big as a baby's dummy. This figure with its useless breasts recalls both the series of women with dead child and the figure with uplifted arms at the right in *Guernica*. The striated patterns, which first appeared the previous summer in Mougins, and which may be seen in a study for *Guernica*, reinforce the drama of the scene. The monstrous woman embodies the suffering of all women oppressed by the barbarity of war.

◁ *Study for a Hand*, 1937, Prado Museum, Madrid

Woman with a Dead Child, 1937, Prado Museum, Madrid

72 *The Supplicant*, 18 December 1937, Paris. Gouache on wood, 24 × 18.5 cm   ▷

73   Women at Their Toilette
Femmes à leur toilette

This huge collage of wallpaper cutouts pasted on beige paper mounted on a canvas support was a tapestry design for Marie Cuttoli, which was finally executed only in 1967.[5] Picasso did not want the cartoon to leave his Grands-Augustins studio—where it occupied the space where he had worked on *Guernica*—and so the transposition would have had to be done there, but this proved to be technically unfeasible. "Picasso was very interested in Marie Cuttoli's work. A number of his canvases had already been reproduced in d'Aubusson tapestry with amazing fidelity. At that particular time, he wanted to make a design specifically intended for a tapestry, and had the idea of using collage techniques. He collected a large quantity of wallpaper from decorators and cut out the shapes of the women's dresses, as well as the hands, faces, and all the other elements of the picture."[6]

In other words, a work that was to serve as a model for a wall-hanging was itself made out of a material used to decorate walls. The collage technique used here differs from that in the Cubist *papiers collés* in that the figural elements are for the most part cut out of single pieces of paper rather than assembled from various fragments, producing an effect not unlike that of Matisse's gouaches. The decorative patterns of the wallpaper are chosen for their formal or material suggestiveness: imitation stonework indicates the background, imitation wood the floor and the frame, floral patterns the flowers. Some of these pieces of wallpaper had already been used for the layout of *Guernica*.

The scene represents a subject that had always been dear to Picasso, and that he had already celebrated in 1906: the toilette. The woman standing on the left combs the hair of the woman in the middle as she looks in the mirror held by the third figure. The likeness reflected in the mirror is not hers, so we might be inclined to see it as a painting. But Picasso, in the *Girl with a Mirror* (1932, The Museum of Modern Art, New York), had already painted a picture in which the model appears in two different forms, her reflection in the mirror be-

ing an imaginary projection or fantasy. This "mirror-picture" in fact illustrates the problems inherent in representational painting. The presence of three women (Olga, Marie-Thérèse and Dora), the date 1938 (right in the midst of the Spanish conflict), and the map designs on one of the dresses endow this apparently ordinary scene from everyday life with a deeper, allegorical meaning.

74   Bust of a Woman with a Striped Hat
Buste de femme au chapeau rayé

During 1938 and 1939, Picasso pushed the disarticulation of the human face to its most extreme limits. The series of portraits of seated women and women with hats—monumental heads shaped like skeins of wool or clumps of straw, with canine muzzles and warped features—constitutes the most devastating assault on the human likeness in all of Picasso's work. The problem, basically, was how to reconcile the expression of the artist's most intense and complex emotions (the psychic rapport between painter and model, Picasso's love-hate relationship with women) and the dramatic events of the time (turmoil in Spain, threat of another war) with the rationality of a formal vocabulary, with the coherence of a pictorial construction involving form and colour, without falling into abstraction, that is, transposing the emotion into another system of signs and images. Picasso achieved this by "splitting up" the figure and endowing it with the power of his own emotivity and spiritual energy, and by creating a new formal vocabulary able to encompass all the dimensions of the artist's aesthetic world and the chaos of history. This is why Picasso concentrated his efforts on the human face—the stage and mirror of the passions—and forced it to conform to the strictures of his pictorial logic. With his fierce sense of humour, his destructive passion and his ironic tenderness, the painter transformed women's faces into "things", all the while giving them an individual expression and character of their own. This is indeed the great paradox of Picasso's painting, and the hallmark of his genius. His "monsters" are human nevertheless, for they give a visible expression to the monstrous and horrible aspects hidden within each one of us. These

73 *Women at Their Toilette*, 1938, Paris. Gouache and printed wallpaper pasted on canvas-mounted paper, 299 x 488 cm "hieratic monarchs, whose strange beauty awakes in us vacillating impressions of amiability, coquetry, mystery, awesomeness, even viciousness",[7] compose the most fantastic portrait-gallery in all of twentieth-century art.

In this *Bust of a Woman with a Striped Hat*, the face has incorporated the graphic qualities of its surroundings: the vertical stripes of the background, the weave of the straw hat, the lines of the hair. In other pictures of the series the figure is built up of basketwork motifs. The head is twisted and broken up into three distinct volumes: a larval form for the mouth and chin, a faceted trapezoid for the forehead, nose and diamond-shaped eye, and a hollowed-out oblong shape for the right profile, which has an unusually large eye. The head rests in precarious equilibrium on a bust with large, round white breasts that are striped with grey in echo of the face. The handling of the nose as a single volume and the multiple viewpoints are close to Cubism, while the disproportions, inverted perspectives and organic permutations derive from the Dinard and Boisgeloup periods. The striped decorative pattern—which often appears during this period—and the wasp-shaped lower part of the face are modelled after the "basketfaces" in the *Dream and Lie of Franco* from 1937. The realistically-rendered expression of the mouth tacked onto this bizarre form, the deep-set, blankly staring eye, the pointed nose, the sweep of hair, and the ridiculous hat with its pyramid and crest, decorated with green foliage (and inscribed with the date), give the figure a peculiarly disquieting expression that suggests stupor. Picasso often said that his principal models at the time were Dora Maar and his dog Kazbek, an Afghan hound with a long muzzle and floppy ears. Quite a few portraits from this period are in fact a combination of the two, the monstrous aspect merging with the animal aspect. This portrait, with its emphatic decorativeness and lively colours, also expresses a certain mordant gaiety, unlike the portraits from the Royan period and the beginning of the war, in which dark grey, green and blue tones and exaggerated distortions suggest a more horrible and tragic reality.

Woman with a Blue Hat, 1939, Musée Picasso, Paris

Female Head, 1939, Musée Picasso, Paris

74 *Bust of a Woman with a Striped Hat*, 3 June 1939, Paris. Oil on canvas, 81 x 54 cm

75 *Maya with a Doll*, 16 January 1938, Paris. Oil on canvas, 73.5 x 60 cm

75 Maya with a Doll
Maya à la poupée

While Fascism continued to gain ground in Spain, and the Munich accords were in the making, Picasso found some consolation in his daughter Maya, born to Marie-Thérèse on 5 October 1935.

The theme of childhood is not a major one in the artist's work, but with each new birth he painted portraits of his children, mostly between the ages of three and seven; after that age he stopped following their development.

His first child, Paulo, was born to Olga in 1921. Maria de la Concepción, named after one of Picasso's sisters who died at the age of seven, was nicknamed Maya. Many years later, he had two more children with Françoise Gilot: Claude in 1947 and Paloma in 1949, when he was 68 years old.

He painted a series of very tender, brightly coloured portraits of Maya, alone with her toys or with her mother. "You see", he once said, "I am not always dwelling on dramatic things."

This painting shows Maya seated on the floor, holding a doll dressed in a sailor's outfit, and this doll is the only "realistically" represented motif in the otherwise very disarticulated portrait. The child has a contented air, with one eye facing forward and the other sideways, a nose shown in profile with both nostrils, a large mouth, and two blonde pigtails tied with ribbons. As in his Cubist period, Picasso shows as many facets of his model as he can. Maya has a surprisingly grown-up face for a three-year-old, almost like her mother's.

76 Man with a Straw Hat and Ice-Cream Cone
Homme au chapeau de paille et au cornet de glace

It was summertime, and ice-cream cones were the latest craze at Mougins. "Everyone was walking around licking his ice, men, women and children alike", Dora Maar recalls. This scene from everyday life inspired a series of male heads executed in a style close to the figures in *Guernica*.

The man in this picture is shown frontally as an assemblage of aggressive decorative patterns, primary signs as in children's drawings. The star-

Head of a Bearded Man, 1938, Musée Picasso, Paris

shaped motif on the cheek recurs on the breasts of Civil War victims in some pictures. The face and hat are full of spiky forms, as if the man had been transformed into a sea-urchin. The neck and collar have sharp, brittle edges. The nostrils, rendered by a figure-eight shape, are enormous for such a tiny nose. The earring adds to the vulgarity of the face. A spiky collar encompasses the base of the rather fragile-looking neck. The hand is fleshy, like a succulent plant. The brutal, hirsute figure is ravenously licking his ice-cream cone, an accessory that will appear the following summer in the hands of Dora Maar and Jacqueline Lamba, André Breton's wife, in the picture titled *Night Fishing at Antibes* (1939, The Museum of Modern Art, New York). The pointed tongue darts out of the sparsely garnished mouth and gives an aggressive sexual connotation to the scene. This man, with his bloodshot eyes and demonic expression, seems quite capable of perpetrating the worst atrocities in warfare. Like universal symbols, similar motifs will appear in the works of the last years.

76 *Man with a Straw Hat and Ice-Cream Cone*, 30 August 1938, Mougins. Oil on canvas, 61 x 46 cm

The War Years

Cat Devouring a Bird, 1939, collection of Mrs. Victor Ganz, New York

Cat, 1943, Musée Picasso, Paris

77   Cat with a Bird in Its Jaws
Chat saisissant un oiseau

Is this an image of the war in Spain, or a premonition of even worse things to come? During the first
three months of 1939, the cities of Madrid, Barcelona and Valencia fell into the hands of Franco's
troops, while Hitler was making inroads into East-
ern Europe. Picasso's mother died on 13 January.
Political and personal events combined in his imagination to find expression in tormented pictures full
of allegorical resonances. Picasso explained: "I
did not paint the war because I am not the kind of
painter who sets out looking for subjects, like a
photographer. But there is no doubt that the war is
present in the paintings that I did at the time. Later,
perhaps, a historian will demonstrate that my work
changed under the influence of the war." From pictures of women mourning the war victims in Spain,
Picasso turned to visions of animals with ferocious
expressions.

   Cat and bird are represented in two different versions: "The subject obsessed me, I don't know
why", the artist later recalled. The cat in this picture
is caked with mud—rendered by the admixture of
sand to the paint—and holds a bird in its jaws. The
bird struggles desperately to free itself from its tormentor's hold. The colour-scheme is muted; dull
browns are punctuated with white streaks that accentuate the cruel claws, the glowing eyes, and the
bird's damaged wing, which shows a raw wound.
The neutrality of the background does nothing to
relieve the horror of the scene: an image from
everyday life blown up to apocalyptic proportions.
The cat "stands menacingly on the threshhold of
the times to come".[1]

77 *Cat with a Bird in Its Jaws*, 22 April 1939, Paris. Oil on canvas, 81 x 100 cm

78 *Boy with a Lobster*, 21 June 1941, Paris. Oil on canvas, 130 x 97.3 cm ▷

78 Boy with a Lobster

Jeune garçon à la langouste

All of the works from the war period express in one way or another the grim and troubled atmosphere that weighed on occupied France. All the catastrophies that denied humanitarian values—massacres, torture, oppression—find a pictorial expression in Picasso's painting. His monstrous figures with deformed, absurd and grotesque faces express his reaction to the "horror of war". A telling anecdote relates that, upon seeing a reproduction of *Guernica* in Picasso's studio, a German officer asked him: "Oh, you did this, Mr. Picasso?" And the artist replied, point blank: "No, you did."

The gallery of horrors constituted by the wartime canvases does not spare children, who are depicted several times, as in such compositions as *Seated Child* from 1939, *Child with Doves* from 1943 (Musée Picasso, Paris), and *The First Steps* from the same year (Yale University Art Gallery, New Haven).

The image of the child effectively combines innocence and monstrosity, cruelty and stupidity, awkwardness and arrogance, victim and tormentor, all the while representing the hope for future life. Here, the child-king sits majestically, brandishing his lobster-sceptre in one hand, with his penis triumphantly displayed below. This "gleeful gnome" with missing teeth is a worthy descendant of Velázquez's dwarves and Murillo's "Bobo". All of Picasso's ongoing pictorial and thematic concerns are summed up in this single image. The sea creatures—blue fish, squid and lobster— are memories of Royan, where Picasso sought refuge during the first year of the war. The child is not at the beach, however, but sitting on a table; this incongruous position, with the penis pointing like a cannon, lends a sarcastic touch to the scene. Not surprisingly in a period when finding provisions was a daily problem, food became one of the leitmotifs in Picasso's painting.

The child's head, with its eye-nose-forehead assemblage, is characteristic of the kind of metamorphosis seen in Picasso's portraits of the period. Here, it is more a matter of pictorial disfiguration than an attempt to represent several different angles or to recompose the features according to a new syntax. The face seems to have been hollowed out, and stretched in opposite directions. This malleability of forms contrasted with the starkly geometrical draughtsmanship illustrates the dual register in which Picasso worked during the forties: supple and swollen forms alternating with rigid geometrical shapes. The frequent striped patterns and grid motifs, which echo the sharply-delineated contours, form a sort of protective shell (symbolized here by the lobster). It is as if Picasso, surrounded by a doomed world, felt an urgent need to condense and solidify forms, to concentrate on blocks.

Note the curious details of the hands: the finger sticking bizarrely out of the palm of one hand, and the stiffly and awkwardly crossed fingers of the

Seated Child, 1939, private collection, United States

Child with Doves, 1943, Musée Picasso, Paris

79 Bull's Head
Tête de taureau

This simple assemblage is one of Picasso's most famous sculptures, and the single best demonstration of his inventive genius and his special relationship with everyday objects. No less interesting than the finished form is the original idea—the combination of two found objects, a bicycle-saddle and handlebars. Works such as these, in which scrap objects are brought together in surprising associations, show that Picasso was always alert and open to whatever was around him, ever ready to transform reality through the play of his imagination. Not only did he collect things with the idea that they "might come in handy someday", but he saw beyond the immediate object itself and sensed the formal implications contained therein, the use to which he could put it in his art. Thus, the handlebars became a pair of horns, the saddle a head. The sculpture is immediately recognizable as a bull's head because Picasso instinctively crystallizes the essential form, the universal archetype that has always represented a bull, from the Lascaux cave-paintings to the children's drawings of today.

Picasso's creativity has something magic, witty and playful about it. He takes objects out of their usual context and miraculously gives them a new function and life. His sculpture is never boring, because he himself was never at a loss for something to do, nor was he ever short of stories to tell. The *Bull's Head* represents the most radical stage of his demiurgic activity and a decisive step in his borrowings from reality in his sculpture. It is also a prefiguration of his works of the fifties, in which a toy automobile will become the head of a baboon, a wicker basket the belly of a goat, a scooter the body of a bird. He had already used actual objects in his sculptures—the spoon in the *Glass of Absinth* (pl. 19), cardboard and leaves in the *Woman with Foliage* (pl. 63), and kitchen utensils for the *Head* (1928, Musée Picasso, Paris) and the *Figure* from 1935 (Musée Picasso, Paris)—inspired sometimes by their original function, sometimes by their form or their material. Henceforth, he combines his previous approaches, choosing the objects for their form, their material, and their meaning, but it is a

other. The muted and thinned out greenish grey and beige colours are in keeping with the atmosphere of sadness that pervades the scene. The visible brushwork is a prefiguration of the violent and sketchy manner of the painter's last period.

displaced, completely new meaning that he invents himself. He would like to take the paradox of illusion even further, so that the bull's head could be "re-viewed" as a bicycle-saddle and handlebars. This is why, even when they are cast in bronze to give the work a unified appearance, the original elements remain identifiable, even if secondary. Picasso had two bronze casts made from the original assemblage; the version usually exhibited and reproduced is in bronze.

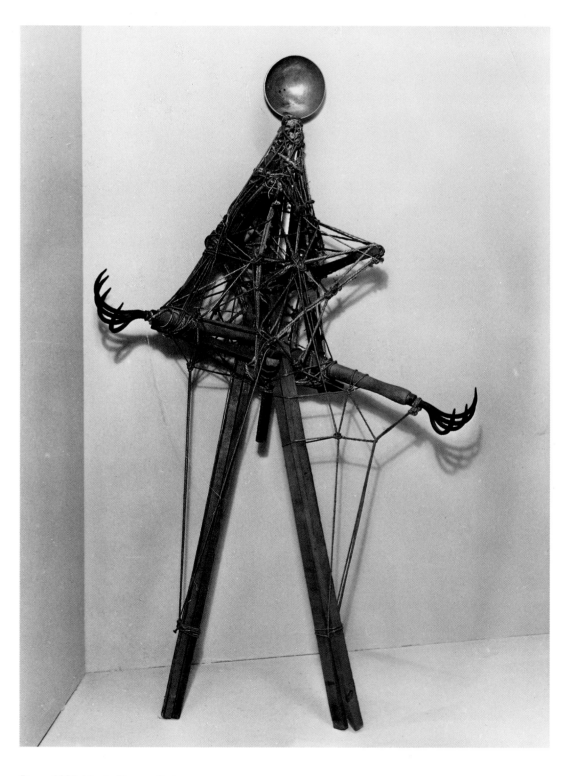

Figure, 1935, Musée Picasso, Paris

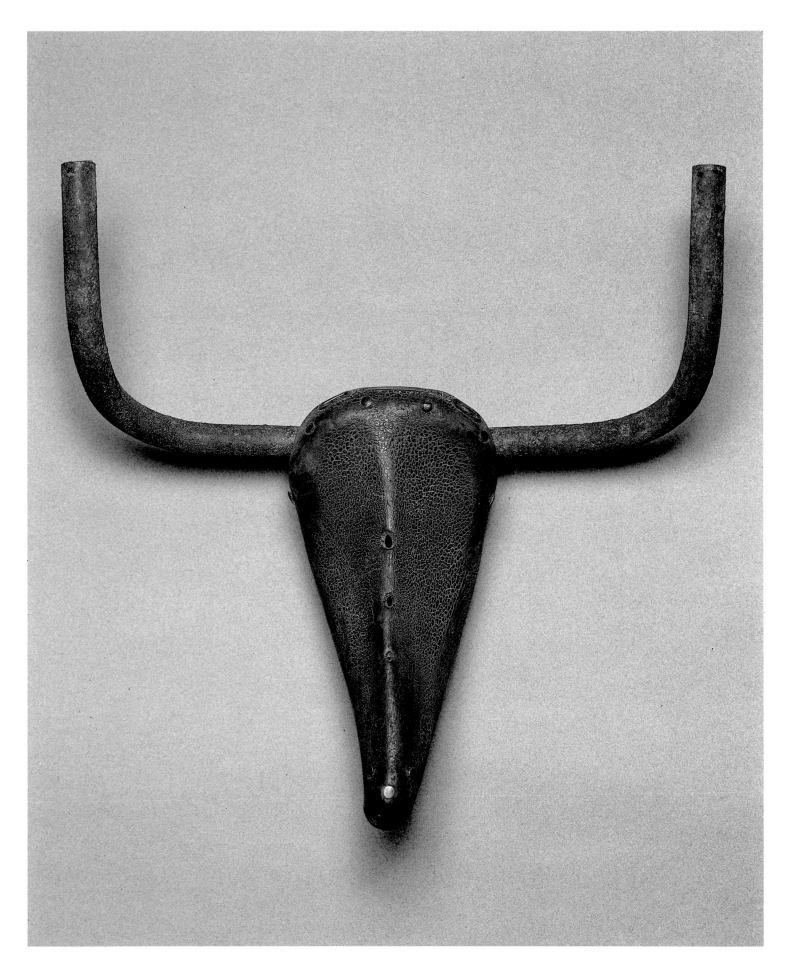

79 *Bull's Head*, spring 1942, Paris. Bicycle-saddle and handlebars (leather, metal), 33.5 x 43.5 x 19 cm

80 The Man with the Sheep

L'homme au mouton

Who is this man carrying a sheep? An antique shepherd from the Mediterranean shores with the animal that he is about to sacrifice to his god? The hieratic, frontal presentation gives him an archaic character that recalls the *moschophoros*, or calf-bearer, on a sixth-century B.C. Greek vase. Or is it the Good Shepherd, holding the sheep who strayed from the fold, firmly grasping its legs in his huge hand? Kahnweiler remarks only that it is "neither ancient nor modern, neither Egyptian, Greek, nor Cubist".[2] Picasso himself denied that the work had any symbolic significance: "The man could just as well be carrying a pig as a sheep! There is no symbolism in it. It is just something beautiful."[3]

It would be tempting to call this a "classical" sculpture. In Picasso's case, and in twentieth-century sculpture in general, that would mean a work of monumental size, entirely modelled in the round; Rodin is often cited as a reference-point in connec-

Studies for "The Man with the Sheep", 1942, Musée Picasso, Paris

Study for "The Man with the Sheep", 1943, Musée Picasso, Paris

80 *The Man with the Sheep*, February/March 1943, Paris. Bronze, 222.5 x 78 x 78 cm ▷

tion with this particular piece. But everything about this statue belies its would-be classicism: the disproportion between certain parts of the body (the hands in particular) and the whole; the sketchy treatment of the legs (whose *non finito* aspect was unintentional, according to Picasso[4]); the lack of balance in the distribution of the volumes (the man holds the animal in front of him, but nothing in his pose expresses this action; this is strikingly apparent in the profile view); the man's "plantigrade" representation, with the body's weight resting equally on both legs, in a statue where traditionally there would have been a *contraposto* (one leg placed in front of the other, with the weight shifted to the back leg).

In the last analysis, however, all interpretations and stylistic considerations aside, "Picasso ends up creating works that stand only for freedom".[5]

81 The Reaper
Le faucheur

André Malraux interpreted this figure as a representation of the Grim Reaper, and imagined it erected in an enlarged version at the tip of the Île Saint-Louis as a monument to Baudelaire, the author of *The Flowers of Evil*[6]. Henri Michaux visualized a more serene and bucolic setting for this little figure "wearing a big straw hat on his head, as round and luminous as the sun in the Midi. [...] When you see something as beautiful as this, it makes you happy for the whole day."[7]

The original was built up out of plaster with a steel armature. A cake-mould pressed into the plaster gave form to the solar head, to which pieces were added for the nose and eyes, and an incision was made for the mouth, giving the face a very lively expression. Malraux asked Jacqueline Picasso if the face had been formed with the mould, and she answered: "Oh no, [Picasso] added it. He almost always modified what he started."[8] The navel is gouged out, arms and legs are grooved. The scythe was another addition, as Jacqueline Picasso recalls: "At first there was no scythe either. Picasso said that the idea just came to him out of the blue."[9]

As Malraux once put it, "every ferment for metamorphosis he made his own".[10] Picasso's involvement in the world was so intense, and he was so keenly attentive to the materials around him, that we are easily fooled. The handle of the scythe is not made out of a paintbrush handle, nor is the body made of twisting vine-branches. The original plaster shows that there was only a worm-eaten piece of wood in the base.

81 *The Reaper*, 1943, Paris. Bronze, 51 x 33.5 x 19.5 cm

Still-Lifes and Vanitas

82 Death's Head
Tête de mort

In occupied Paris all bronze statues were requisitioned to be melted down and used for weapons. But Picasso, with the aid of friends, was able to hide some metal and have his works cast at night in a clandestine forge.

The motif of the death's head recurs frequently in his painting and sculpture from the war years. The skulls are not conventionally skeletal, but crude masses shot with gaping holes. It is the age-old theme of the *memento mori*, the reminder of the brevity of life.

The *Death's Head* from 1943, modelled out of a single solid block, is larger than lifesize and, like the small bronze animals that Picasso had been making since the beginning of the war, has no base; it is the absence of spatial points of reference that gives it its monumental character. The forehead is smooth, the cheeks deeply scored. The contours of the eyes, or rather the hollow eyesockets, are neatly defined, but the nasal cavity seems to have been torn open. The mouth has the appearance of having been stitched up, with something like scar tissue forming over it; it seems to want to cry out,

82 *Death's Head*, Paris. 1943,
Bronze and copper,
25 x 21 x 31 cm

83 *Skull, Sea-Urchins and Lamp on a Table*, 27 November 1946, Antibes/Paris. Oil on plywood, 81 x 100 cm

Vanitas, 1946,
Musée des
Beaux-Arts, Lyons

to reveal countless horrors, as if the sightless skull had witnessed the passage of our entire history.

This *Death's Head* contrasts with the calm strength of *The Man with the Sheep* from the same year (pl. 80), which stands as the hopeful vision of a renewal. In the former, the smooth surfaces give no hold to the light that dances over it, while in the latter the rough texture imprisons pockets of light.

83   Skull, Sea-Urchins and Lamp on a Table
Crâne, oursins et lampe sur une table

During the Second World War Picasso painted a great number of still-lifes, as many as during the Cubist period. They present skulls and various other objects, and "are dominated by the theme of humble everyday life".[1] Since the beginning of 1946 Picasso had been in the habit of transforming skulls into owls, because of the visual analogy (large round eyes, etc.). Sea-urchins are a frequent adjunct.

In this canvas painted after the liberation, the skull, with its sarcastic expression and ambiguous grin, seems to turn on itself to show all of its facets. It sits next to a phallic-shaped oil-lamp; the flame has gone out, as fragile and fleeting as life. (This type of lamp was widely used at the time instead of candles.) There is a plate of sea-urchins—Picasso spent the summer of 1946 at the Palais Grimaldi in Antibes, and we know that crustaceans often symbolize cruelty in his work. The whole ensemble breathes the vanity of life. The grey, black, white and yellow colours reinforce the macabre atmosphere, which is unrelieved by the flat handling and the black outlines around the objects. The light is fragmented into facets that structure the painting, a distant reminder of the Cubist period.

84   The Kitchen
La cuisine

In November 1948 Picasso painted two slightly different versions of *The Kitchen*, both monumental, monochrome, and virtually abstract. In her memoirs, Francoise Gilot tells the story of their making: "Pablo executed the first version of a large-format painting called *The Kitchen*, which was inspired by the kitchen at the Rue des Grands-Augustins in which we sometimes ate our evening meal. The room was painted all in white, and, apart from the usual utensils, there were two birdcages in it. The only accents of colour were the three Spanish plates hung on the walls. The kitchen was basically an empty white cube, enlivened only by the birds and the colourful plates. Pablo told me one evening: 'I am going to make a painting of that—that is to say, of nothing.' And that's exactly what he did. He drew a network of lines to structure the space and added a few concentric lines to create target-like shapes—the Spanish plates. In the background one could just make out the owl and the turtledoves. At this stage of the work he looked at the canvas and declared: 'I now see two possible directions for this canvas. Let's make a second version of it, exactly the same, and I will take it from there.'"[2]

The first version, the simplest and most extreme, was thus little more than a linear framework organizing the space. Picasso, however, felt the need to give some pictorial nourishment to this rather dry composition, and in the second version (pl. 84) he added coloured details such as the succulent plant on the right, the patterns of the plates, and the silhouettes of the three birds with the cage. Within and behind the framework of dots and lines he added splashes of colour whose shape and arrangement give depth and relief to the picture. The lines are independent of the background; they create a surface pattern that rhythmically articulates and contains the spatial tension. "Form", Picasso liked to say, "is a hollow volume against which the outside pressure is such that it produces the appearance of an apple . . . . It is the rhythmic pressure of space on this form that matters."[3]

This spatial draughtmanship recalls the wire constructions of 1928. The motif of dots and lines first appears in the abstract drawings of constellations from 1924. It is also found in a condensed form in the illustrations for Reverdy's *Song of the Dead*, which was published in 1943. This specific pictorial "handwriting", which was according to some, derived from simplified bone shapes and, according to others, inspired by designs on Gallic coins, became the basis for many pictorial variations during

84 *The Kitchen*, November 1948, Paris. Oil on canvas, 175 x 252 cm the fifties. It is used in a tighter, more closely-knit manner in the lithographs, and more loosely in the ceramic works, like the framework of a new pictorial language. Picasso never got bogged down in abstraction: when he invented a new system of graphic representation, it was not to demonstrate it just for its own sake, but to put it immediately to the test of figuration, to confront it with another mode of expression.

85   Goat's Skull, Bottle and Candle
Crâne de chèvre, bouteille et bougie

Once again, Picasso turns to the painted sculpture, combining two techniques that he had used alternately, each referring invariably to the other in a dialogue that began with Cubism and was reactivated by the artist's constant technical innovations. This *Goat's Skull, Bottle and Candle* belongs to a series of painted bronzes that goes back to the *Glass of Absinth* of 1914 (pl. 19). It is midway between the assemblage-sculptures incorporating found objects—here, bicycle handlebars and nails —the "cast textures" (the imprint of corrugated cardboard for the head) and the painted sheet metal works of the later years. It is the three-dimensional projection of still-lifes of similar composition painted during these years.[4] Colour plays an active and decisive role in the definition of the planes and in the work's expressivity: it functions not only as an element of decoration, but also as a structural element. The decomposition of the bottle into curved surfaces formed by a pair of roof-tiles, which gives such a novel impression of volume and space, is a direct consequence of Cubism. *Goat's Skull, Bottle and Candle* may be regarded as "the compendium of Picasso's pictorial resources: the bottle refers to the problem of open, transparent sculpture, as it was formulated in the *Glass of Absinth* from 1914; the metal armature that suggests volume recalls the sculptures made with González; and the use of the handlebars to represent horns alludes to the ingenious *Bull's Head*. The hair on top of the goat's head is suggested by a cluster of small nails; longer nails are used to represent the beams of candlelight; the texture of the skull, obtained by making an imprint of corrugated cardboard in

plaster, is related to the Boisgeloup sculptures, in which such techniques were used to replace conventional modelling. The eyes are made with steel buttons."[5]

The sculpture is composed of two distinct masses, one vertical and open—the bottle—and the other horizontal and compact—the skull. Picasso depicts the traditional iconography of the *vanitas* still-life, which opposes symbols of light and life to symbols of death. The *memento mori* theme illustrated by an ox's or goat's skull was inaugurated in 1908 in a painting commemorating the death of the poet Wiegels; it reappeared later, in 1942, on the occasion of the death of González, and may also be seen in the 1958 *Still-Life with Bull's Skull* (pl. 95). The present work may have been inspired by the the death of Picasso's friend, the poet Paul Éluard, in November 1952.

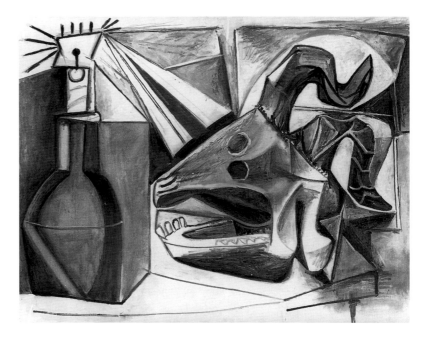

Goat's Skull, Bottle and Candle, 1952, Musée Picasso, Paris

85   *Goat's Skull, Bottle and Candle*, 1951–53, Vallauris. Painted bronze, 79 x 93 x 54 cm

Sculpture and Assemblage

86   The Woman with the Pushchair
La femme à la poussette

In 1949 Picasso rented some old pottery ware-houses in the Rue du Fournas in Vallauris and set up three workshops: one for painting, one for sculpture, and one for ceramics. Here he collected all sorts of scrap objects and materials: tiles, stones, baskets, bits of metal, etc. The large sculptures of 1949-51, which mark his return to a naturalistic style in three-dimensional work, were made from assemblages of these odds and ends.

The Woman with the Pushchair was built up around a real baby-carriage. The figure of the child is composed of pieces of pottery. The mother, who stands tall and straight on high-heel shoes, has a skirt made out of a rolled sheet of metal, a corsage made out of stoveplates, and cake-moulds for breasts. Starting from a scene that he often observed in his everyday life—Françoise perambulating Claude—Picasso succeeded in transforming apparently incongruous elements into a monument to motherhood that is not without humour.

87   The Goat
La chèvre

This goat with bloated udder could be Amalthea, who nursed Zeus. But the goat was also a familiar companion of the artist's everyday life (at La Californie, his home in Cannes, there was a goat he had received as a Christmas present; in a photograph taken by David Douglas Duncan[1] we can see it attached by a chain to the tail of its bronze counterpart).

Using diverse materials and objects that he found around him or specifically chose for their shape or texture, Picasso, the master scavenger, built up the basic form of the goat. One section of a slightly whittled palm-branch made the backbone, another the forehead; an old wicker basket be-

came the belly, pieces of wood (with knots that look just like joints) and bits of metal were used for the legs, and a piece of twisted iron rod for the tail. Around this frail armature held together by wire and supported by a pile of bricks he fashioned the rest of the animal, partially covering the assembled objects with plaster and adding details: pieces of vine-branches for the horns and "goatee", cardboard for the ears, a tin can for the sternum, two earthenware milk-jugs with their handles removed for the udder, a piece of metal folded in half to make the vulva, and a short piece of tubing for the anus. Here and there, a flat piece of wood or iron bar was used to accentuate a surface or a projecting edge. The figure was then cast in bronze.

Picasso's approach to assembling these found objects and materials was at once very light-hearted and very serious. "With Picasso this act, which could have been done purely in jest, instead took on the mysterious gravity of a sacred ritual imposed upon him by some unknown religion."[2]

Like the mythical Pyrrha and Deucalion, who re-populated the earth with men and women by casting away the stones they picked up on the road, Picasso's hand gave new life to the objects that he found by the wayside.

Baboon with its Child, 1952, Musée Picasso, Paris

88 Little Girl Skipping
Petite fille sautant à la corde

The *Little Girl Skipping*, like *The Woman with the Pushchair* (pl. 87), is a humorous and fanciful combination of modelling and assemblage. This seemingly weightless, free-floating sculpture, which is unusual both as to subject and technique, has fittingly been described as the "sardonic denial of statuary".[3]

"Pablo Picasso had always dreamed of making a sculpture that did not touch the ground", Françoise Gilot explains. "He found the solution watching a little girl skipping. He had a metalworker in Vallauris make a rectangular base on which he set up a length of iron pipe that stood about a meter high and that had been bent to look like a skipping rope when it touches the ground. The ends of this 'rope' served as a support for the figure of the little girl. The body was made with a shallow basket of the kind used to gather orange-blossoms for the perfume factories. It was connected to the tubing with a wooden grip on each side. Underneath the basket Pablo put some heavy crumpled paper and

Little Girl Skipping, Vallauris, 1950, Picasso Archives

poured plaster over it. When the plaster was dry he removed the paper, and there was the skirt. He then added two legs carved out of wood, to the ends of which he attached two shoes found at the junkyard (both for the same foot), which he had filled with plaster. For the face he used the cover of a box of chocolates, which he also filled with plaster. When the plaster had dried he took the cover away and stuck this shape on a plaster rectangle he had textured with a piece of corrugated cardboard, one end of which was narrowed to form the neck. Oblique cuts were made on either side to give the impression of hair falling on the shoulders."[4]

The assemblage of found objects into new combinations, which began with the 1935 *Figure* (Musée Picasso, Paris), and was followed by the famous *Bull's Head* of 1942 (pl. 79), attains a striking unity in this work and takes on a further dimension thanks to the technique of modelling in plaster to harmonize the various elements. The work was later cast in bronze, a process that guarantees its preservation, but somewhat negates the specific qualities of the very different materials used. Picasso's sculpture-assemblages are rich in expressive anecdotal details that reveal shrewd psychological insight. Here, the short skirt, oversize shoes, neatly-combed hair and doll-like face evoke the right degree of stiltedness and gaucheness to create an archetypal "little girl" figure. Picasso was fascinated by the mixture of the playful, the innocent and the perverse in such creatures, and the terror and tenderness they inspired in him are evinced in the play *The Four Little Girls* that he wrote in 1947/48.

87 *The Goat*, 1950, Vallauris. Plaster, 120 x 72 x 144 cm

◁ **86** *The Woman with the Pushchair*, 1950, Vallauris. Bronze, 203 x 145 x 61 cm

The Fifties

89 Child Playing with a Toy Truck
Enfant jouant avec un camion

When Françoise Gilot left him in September 1953, Picasso found himself all alone in Vallauris, but the children came to spend their Christmas vacation with him. This gave him the occasion to observe their activities with that much more poignancy. Like Goya, Reynolds and Renoir, he was a painter who sought to express the entire range of emotions inspired by children: tenderness, fragility, innocence, cruelty, revery and play.

In this picture he represents Claude playing with a toy truck. In another picture with a similar subject,[1] the scene with Claude is in the background, while in the foreground we see the artist sketching. During this period, Picasso often painted two versions of an identical subject, introducing slight variations. In this, the second version, the child is placed at lower left, bending over his toy, and the

In Front of the Garden, 1953, Zervos, 16:97

rest of the pictorial space is occupied by a decorative plant motif.[2] With its bold composition, the painting looks like the blow-up of a detail of the first version—an unusual procedure for Picasso. The bright colours and decorative patterns are close to the works of Matisse.

90 The Shadow
L'ombre

Many works from 1953 are dark, hermetic and full of solitude. The separation from Françoise and the children was perhaps one of the most severe crises in the artist's personal life, and it was to have profound aesthetic consequences. In fewer than three months Picasso produced no fewer than 154 drawings on the subject of the painter and his model that "summarize in a bitter, ironic, and implacable manner the absurd drama of creation, the indissociable duality between art and life, and between art and love. Woman is there to be painted, but she must also be loved, and the artist, however much genius he may have, is no less a mortal man, and there-

Picasso, Paloma, Maya, Claude and Paulo at La Galloise, Vallauris, 25 December 1953, photograph by Edward Quinn

◁ **88** *Little Girl Skipping*, 1950, Vallauris. Wicker basket, cake-mould, shoes, wood, iron, pottery and plaster, 152×65×66 cm

89 *Child Playing with a Toy Truck*, 27 December 1953, Vallauris. Oil on canvas, 130 x 96.5 cm

90 *The Shadow*, 29 December 1953, Vallauris. Oil and charcoal on canvas, 129.5 x 96.5 cm

Nude in the Studio, 1953, private collection, Switzerland

fore subject to old age, illness and death."[3] *The Shadow* and the *Nude in the Studio*,[4] both painted within the same twenty-four-hour period, are the introduction to this new phase of creativity.

In the present painting, Picasso represents himself as a shadow looking at a nude woman, an "imaginary model"[5] (Françoise), half-real, half-canvas, reclining in the bedroom at La Galloise. The woman's head is tiny, her hand disproportionately large; her pose is full of sensual abandon, the arms thrown back behind the head. Perhaps she is sleeping; Picasso liked to watch women in their sleep, lost to the world. "It was our bedroom. Do you see my shadow? I had just turned away from the window; you see my shadow and the sunlight falling on the bed and floor? You see the toy cart on the dresser and the little vase on the mantel? They come from Sicily, and they're still in the house", the artist explained to David Douglas Duncan.[6]

91 Jacqueline with Crossed Hands
Jacqueline aux mains croisées

This portrait, painted on the same day as its pendant, *Jacqueline with Flowers*,[7] celebrates the entry of Picasso's new companion, Jacqueline Roque, into his painting. Antonina Vallentin calls the figure a "modern sphinx", and it is true that in this crouching position, with her long neck and almond-shaped eyes, Jacqueline has something of the mythic figure about her. She liked this particular

position for sitting, and it will be seen again in later portraits,[8] including the "Odalisques" series. When Picasso first met her, he was struck by her resemblance to the woman with the hookah in Delacroix's *Women of Algiers* (1834, Musée du Louvre, Paris). He saw in her the same classical, Mediterranean type of beauty that he had begun to paint in Gósol. In one portrait of Jacqueline with a black kerchief on her head,[9] she looks like a direct descendant of the Catalan peasant-women of 1906.

The present portrait comes after the series of heads of Sylvette and drawings of Geneviève Laporte, and shows affinities to these. The body is an angular block, with a few yellow stripes indicating the clothes. The background is divided into geometric areas filled in with visible brushstrokes, and the floor is represented by a pattern of lozenges.

The portrait and its pendant were exhibited at the Maison de la Pensée Française in July 1954 with the title *Portrait of Madame Z.*, Picasso's code-name for Jacqueline, who lived at the time in a house called Villa Ziquet. His faithful companion and model from 1954 to 1973, she features prominently in his late paintings.

Jacqueline with Flowers, 1954, private collection

92 Bacchanalia
Bacchanale

Mythological subjects appear periodically in Picasso's work. The series of drawings done in Cannes between 15 September and 13 October 1955[10] presents two themes: the rape of Deianeira, Heracles' wife, by the centaur Nessos—on which he had already done six variations at Juan-les-Pins in 1920—and the Poussinesque bacchanalia, which recalls the processions of maenads and sileni drawn at Cannes in 1933.

This particular drawing, one of the highlights of the retrospective held at the Grand-Palais in 1966/67, is unquestionably the masterpiece of the series from the autumn of 1955. The first two studies show the familiar groups of youthful musicians playing their enchanting melodies for the rounds of dancers. In the third, presented here, we see Silenus embracing an ecstatic maenad with tambourine and triumphantly brandishing his thyrsus, while a drunken faun sprawls at his feet. Nearby, a flutist blows with all his might into his instrument to celebrate the feast of the flesh. The scene takes place at night; the body of the woman is highlighted with gouache and glows milky-white in the moonlight, and one can almost hear the laughter and the incessant music. There is a strange blend of triviality and poetry in the figures: the coarse laughter, triumphant gesture and obscene attitude of the wood-god, the drunken stupor of the faun sprawled on the ground; then again the closed eyes and pleasure-hungry body of the entranced woman and the rapt concentration of the musician. There is also a striking contrast between the fleshy, muscular/voluptuous bodies of the couple, with the distortions and exaggerations of proportion, and the more subdued handling of the fauns. The baroque mastery of the drawing makes it a worthy descendant of Rubens's best works in the genre.

92 *Bacchanalia*, 22/23 September 1955, Cannes. Indian ink and wash with white gouache, 50 x 65.5 cm

93 The Studio at La Californie
L'atelier de La Californie

In 1955 Picasso had moved to a new house in Cannes called La Californie, a huge mansion built during the Belle-Époque and surrounded by a lush and exotic garden. He set up his studio in the vast living-room and transformed this baroque and lavishly decorated setting into a "stage" for the act of painting. This move marked his definitive establishment on the Mediterranean coast, which had been prepared by extended sojourns at Golfe-Juan, Antibes and Vallauris. The atmosphere and decor of La Californie inspired a series of pictures on the theme of the studio, which Picasso himself called "interior landscapes". Between October 1955 and November 1956 he painted over a dozen canvases on the subject, ranging in mood from a colourful and decorative Mediterranean exuberance to a more austere "Spanish" severity. This painting is midway between the two in feeling.

The traditional theme of the studio—which, like that of the artist and model, offers scope for "painting within painting"—may here be seen as a homage to Matisse, a belated response to his studio series from 1911-13 (and also to Braque's paintings on the same theme of a slightly earlier date). Matisse, who died in 1954, had already made his presence felt in the "Women of Algiers" series after Delacroix, a true celebration of colour, orientalism and the odalisque; an echo can be seen here in the portrait of Jacqueline in a Turkish costume at lower right.

The long, uninterrupted dialogue between the two painters, which had expressed itself in both oppositions and convergences, here finds its final and most exemplary manifestation. The entire painting is a compendium of references to Matisse, an "inventory of his pictorial signs":[11] the black background, the luminous white of the patches of bare canvas, the decorative arabesques of the Moroccan coffee-table and the palm-trees, the interplay of positive and negative forms in the windows and shutters, the flat expanses of gentle colour, and, finally, the space completely devoid of human presence, inhabited only by the silence of painting.

The villa's interior and furnishings are easily recognizable: the bronze sculpture, the little stepped stool, the brown wardrobe, the Art Nouveau designs of the windows, which often inspired Picasso to variations. As in Courbet's *Studio*, the centre of the picture is occupied by a canvas on an easel, but here the canvas is in its virgin state—yet pregnant with all manner of possibilities.

When Alfred Barr spoke of the Spanish influence in the dark brown and greyish black colours in another depiction of this subject, Picasso said simply: "Velázquez". And indeed, here we have a premonition of the "Meninas" series, studio pictures par excellence, which were also painted at La Californie: the canvas is in place, the axes have been drawn, the stage is set.

93 *The Studio at La Californie*, 30 March 1956, Cannes. Oil on canvas, 114 x 146 cm

94   The Bathers
Les baigneurs

Picasso revolutionized every aspect of the art of sculpture. In *The Bathers* he dealt with the problem of making compositions with several figures, and created a coherent, integrated group. On the formal level they are prefigurations of his flat, geometric style in sculpture. The six figures stand like rectilinear posts, the rhythmic interplay deriving from the disks, squares, rhomboids and obliques of the heads and arms.

The original models were made of coarse wooden planks nailed together. As he had done many times before, the artist incorporated *objets trouvés*: broomhandles, pieces of a shovel, legs of a bed. In the bronze version, however, these individual elements lose their identity and exist purely for their formal function and their ability to harmonize within the composition of the figures as a whole.

Despite the formal rigour, which was to inspire many sculptors of the sixties, Picasso remained attached to psychological realism and the representation of scenes. Each figure has its own distinct personality. By assembling a few odd pieces of wood, Picasso could create a living figure. This use of wood had its origin in the constructions of the Cubist period and later reappeared in smaller sculptures like *The Jar-Carrier* from 1935 (Musée Picasso, Paris). The same principle was used in several later works, including the *Man with a Javelin, Head*, and *Figure* from 1958.[12]

The Diver, 1956,
Musée Picasso,
Paris

*The Man with
Joined Hands*, 1956,
Musée Picasso,
Paris

94 *The Bathers*, summer 1956, Cannes. Bronze

95 Still-Life with Bull's Skull
Nature morte à la tête de taureau

This composition was painted at La Californie between two stages of work on *The Bay of Cannes* (Musée Picasso, Paris). The dates inscribed on the back of the canvas—28 to 30 May, and 7 and 9 June—correspond to the culmination of the political crisis in France occasioned by the revolt in Algeria and De Gaulle's takeover of the government. Pierre Daix[13] associates this climate of anxiety and violence with the reoccurrence in Picasso's work of the bull's skull motif, which appears as a theme in itself in a series of drawings[14] beginning in April, and subsequently in a number of large canvases.[15] This *Still Life with Bull's Skull*, which is directly related to the depiction of the theme in the Düsseldorf still-life that commemorates the death of González in 1942, is both the largest painting in the series and its conclusion.

The contrast between life and death in this picture is like a "bolt from the blue". The unsettling presence of the decapitated head with its vacant orbits and stark jaw strikes a morbid note, which is however belied by other features such as the bouquet of lilies-of-the-valley, the sunburst motifs, and the bright colours, all of which give a feeling of light and life. The sunfilled window, which constitutes a marked architectonic frame within the composition, is that of Picasso's studio at La Californie. He obviously loved the view of the coast and sea from this window, since it appears in a number of paintings, not as a landscape, but rather as a picture within a picture.

Pierre Daix has interpreted the red, white and blue chromaticism as a patriotic statement, on the lines of the French flags that Picasso depicted first in a 1918 drawing (Musée Picasso, Paris), and again in 1945, during the liberation of Paris.

The La Californie period (and later the Vauvenargues period) is characterized by the adoption of a new pictorial technique that makes full use of the possibilities of the oil medium, playing on contrasts between strongly saturated colours and extremely diluted ones. Very likely influenced by the works of Dubuffet and the Action Painters, Picasso gives free rein to his materials and to textural effects—drips, splashes, crisp brushstrokes. He lets painting take its own course and "seeks in the pictorial medium its material truth".[16]

The impasto, the play of transparency in the layers of colour, and the integration of thick, hardened chunks of paint on the canvas anticipate the technique of certain late works.

Still-Life with Bull's Skull, 1942, Kunstsammlung Nordrhein-Westfalen, Düsseldorf

95 *Still-Life with Bull's Skull*, 25 May–9 June 1958, Cannes. Oil on canvas, 162.5 x 130 cm

The Last Years

96 The Luncheon on the Grass
Le déjeuner sur l'herbe

"When I see Manet's *Déjeuner sur l'herbe*, I tell myself: tribulations for later", Picasso once wrote on the back of an envelope.[1] This significant and prophetic statement is revelatory of the profundity and fecundity of the Picasso/Manet dialogue. Throughout his career Picasso took inspiration from works of the past; at a number of decisive moments in his development he felt the need to confront his predecessors, to explore a theme, a motif from the universal repertory of art. The "Déjeuner" series, which was begun in August 1959 and completed in July 1962, was the last of his interpretations of old masters, following those of Delacroix's *Femmes d'Alger* in 1955 and Velázquez's *Las Meninas* in 1957. It is also the longest-running and richest set of such variations: in all, it comprises 27 paintings, 140 drawings, a few linocuts and about ten cardboard models for sculptures. The series falls into several distinct phases, each culminating in a "definitive" version proceeding from dozens of sketches and drawings that constitute what Douglas Cooper calls "the laboratory of the image".[2]

In this particular version Picasso respects the positions of the figures and the setting (trees, clearing, river), the dominant blue, green and pink colour-scheme, and such details as the still-life in the foreground. He has left out one of the men, however, to lay more weight on the relationship between the man talking on the right and the monumental woman seated on the left, a confrontation that re-evokes the oft-treated dialogue between the painter and his model. In these stylistic exercises Picasso uses the original for his own purposes, but without radically upsetting its general structure. Each set of interpretations corresponds to a different style, as if he wanted to check his formal innovations against a well-defined model. Here, the tight, cursive stroke allows the figures to be inte-

Le Dejeuner sur l'herbe, after Manet, 1961, Musée Picasso, Paris

Le Déjeuner sur l'herbe, after Manet, Mougins, 12 July 1961, Musée Picasso, Paris

Edouard Manet, *Le Déjeuner sur l'herbe*, 1863, Musée d'Orsay, Paris ▷

96   *The Luncheon on the Grass*, 3 March–20 August 1960, Vauvenargues. Oil on canvas, 130 x 195 cm

grated into the decorative background, and there is a swirling impasto texture; in other versions the line is schematic and stiff, the figures flat like shapes cut out of cardboard.

One might well wonder what there was in this work that appealed so much to Picasso that he explored it with such insistence. For one thing, the subject gave him the opportunity to tackle landscape, the challenge of suggesting the coolness of the spot, the filtered light in the woods, and the fluidity of matter. The presence of nudes in an outdoor setting is a response to such works as Cézanne's *Large Bathers* and Matisse's *Joie de Vivre* (1906, Barnes Foundation, Merion, Pa.). From Cézanne he learned to incorporate figures in a landscape, to create a solid architecture for the whole; from Matisse he took the idyllic pastoral atmosphere.

97 Woman with Outstretched Arms
Femme aux bras écartés

The series of painted sheet metal figures from the sixties, the last phase of Picasso's three-dimensional explorations, develops and systematizes the principle of flat sculpture first expounded in *The Bathers* (pl. 94). These works integrate to an even greater degree such specifically pictorial components as the plane surface and colour. "Sculpture is the best commentary that a painter can make on painting", Picasso once said. "To get a sculpture, all you have to do is to cut out your painting."[3] Statements such as these show that Picasso was constantly aware of the dialogue between the two modes of expression.

To make this type of figure, he began by cutting a piece of paper or cardboard and folding it to create planes, which would give a spatial orientation and suggest volume. The model was then transposed onto a sheet of metal that was also folded and painted white or coloured. This use of folded and painted metal recalls the *Violin* from 1915 (pl. 20) and the *Guitar* from 1925 (Musée Picasso, Paris), except that Picasso is now more concerned

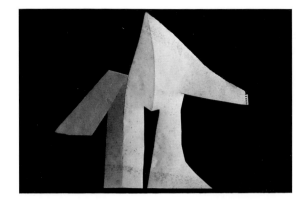

Model for "Woman with Outstretched Arms", 1961, Musée Picasso, Paris

with formal simplification—surface continuity rather than internal structure. Space is no longer within, but all around. There are no more intersections or juxtapositions of planes, just a continuous surface of angular or curved contour. Starting from a technique within the reach of any child—cutting out and folding—Picasso was able to create a world of monumental metal figures as diverse as the *Woman with a Child*, the *Seated Pierrot* (Musée Picasso, Paris), and the "Footballers". The *Women with Outstretched Arms*, with her tiny head, arms extended like wings, and triangular shape, looks like a great bird that is about to fly away. As in all of these sheet metal sculptures, there is an impression of lightness. Anatomical details are indicated in black; the grating used around the head and limbs serves to represent shadows and to make the figure stand out in greater relief. In this particular figure Picasso plays on various textural effects to animate the surface, but in others he uses only paint. An enlarged version of this sculpture, made of concrete and originally destined for Kahnweiler's garden at the priory of Saint-Hilaire, was donated by Louise and Michel Leiris to the Musée National d'Art Moderne, and is now on permanent loan at the Picasso Museum.

Woman with a Child, 1961, Musée Picasso, Paris

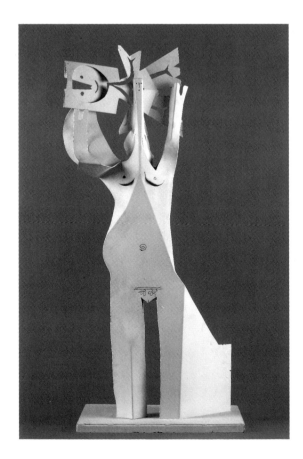

97 *Woman with Outstretched Arms*, 1961, Cannes. Painted sheet metal with grating, 183 x 177 x 72.5 cm

98 The Kiss
Le baiser

The theme of the couple, omnipresent throughout Picasso's career, became virtually an obsession toward the end of his life.

The realism of the tender or violent scenes of kissing couples, usually portrayed without a decor, shows how much importance sexual love had for the artist. This *Kiss* from 1969 shows two heads joined by a single line occupying the entire pictorial space. Picasso does not hesitate to deform the faces in order to bring them closer together: "Of the two, he makes but one, to express the intimate fusion that takes place during the act of kissing."[4] The noses mould themselves into a mutual contour; the mouths bite each other; the woman's eyes, both of which are visible even though she is shown in profile, have moved up her forehead, which is tilted back. All the paintings of this period that represent couples illustrate the same fusion of two beings. The man is old and balding, and has a long beard; his eyes are wide open, as if he were having a revelation; he is bigger than the woman and seems gentle and protective. Gone is the erotic frenzy of the sexual act in former years (pl. 32); expressed here is the tenderness and serenity of Picasso's years with Jacqueline. Subsequently, the theme of the couple was to take on a more pathetic aspect, as in the impotent old man in the *Nude Man and Woman* from 1971 (Mr. and Mrs. Raymond D. Nasher Collection).[5]

99 Woman with a Pillow
Femme à l'oreiller

Concurrent with his audacious pictorial exploits, Picasso continued working in a vein that could be called "classical": consider this seated nude painted virtually in black and white. This type of colour-scheme, with its touches of grey and ivory, is rare in Picasso's work. One has to go back as far as 1923, to paintings like *Olga in a Fur Collar* (Musée des Beaux-Arts, Lille) or *The Idyll* (Marina Picasso Collection), to find similar harmonies. In the present case, white is not used to cover other colours, but directly as the dominant tonality. Picasso made many preparatory drawings for this splendid

Bust of Reclining Woman, 1969, Zervos, 31:312

Reclining Nude, 1969, Zervos, 31:311

Reclining Nude, 1967, Musée Picasso, Paris

100 Reclining Nude and Man Playing the Guitar
Nu couché et homme jouant de la guitare

This painting belongs to what has been called the Avignon Period (1969 - 72), because of the two major exhibitions at the Palais des Papes in 1970 and 1973 that presented many of Picasso's late works.

This final phase represents a contribution to Western painting equal in importance to that of Cubism, though in another domain. It stands not only as the apotheosis of a lifetime devoted to creation and the artistic testament of a genius, but also as the source of new pictorial possibilities, an opening toward a renewal of figuration, an apology for the new-found lyrical power of the painted image. This period was for a long time decried, because it was misunderstood by an entire generation of critics who had sworn allegiance to a strict, post-Matissian formalism, and saw it only as the obsessive indulgence of an aging painter from a bygone era. It has since been accorded its due,[9] and in the eighties it played the same seminal role in the development of art that Matisse's paper cutouts had in the decade between 1965 and 1975.[10]

Toward the end of his life, Picasso seems to have reconnected with his Spanish roots: the subject-matter, the atmosphere, the manner of painting, all have a strong Hispanic flavour. Matadors, men with swords, guitarists, watermelon-eaters are the typical figures of this world of what Malraux calls "tarots". The dominant colour-schemes are harmonies of greys and black with startling accents of bright orange, golden yellow and pink. The "baroqueness", the preposterous humour and derision, and the tragic awareness of death that pervades these works makes them worthy descendants of those of Velázquez and Goya.

In this picture Picasso returns to a theme he had already treated in a number of variations, the serenade, a theme that combines music and love: a man playing the flute or guitar and a nude woman are joined by the bond of a musical homage. The guitar here looks like a gourd, and its analogy with the forms of the woman's body attests to the affinity that Picasso always had for this instrument; for him, the guitar was associated both with the

portrait of Jacqueline in which he carefully worked out the details of the face[6] and the half-seated, half-reclining position on the lace-trimmed pillow[7] that recalls Goya's *Naked Beauty* (*Maja desnuda*). The strong expressivity of the face comes from the almost natural-seeming inset of the profile in the frontal view. The monumental aspect of the woman's body in this frontal view confirms that "Jacqueline has the gift of becoming painting to an unimaginable degree".[8] Jacqueline Picasso was so fond of this painting that she bought it back from the Louise Leiris gallery.

98 *The Kiss*, 26 October 1969, Mougins. Oil on canvas, 97 x 130 cm

99 *Woman with a Pillow*, 10 July 1969, Mougins. Oil on canvas, 194 x 130 cm ▷

100   *Reclining Nude and Man Playing the Guitar*, 1970, Mougins. Oil on canvas, 130 x 195 cm

cante jondo of his Andalusian childhood and with the female anatomy. This work displays all of the pictorial characteristics of the Avignon period: crudely drawn forms, elementary graphic cyphers (fishbone pattern for the woman's sex, spirals for the man's beard), and enormous fan-shaped feet and hands. The form of the heads, with their prominent noses, recalls the Boisgeloup period. The woman's body is twisted and pressed flat against the picture plane so that all the parts may be seen.

The paint is thickly applied, worked up in some areas and briskly handled in others, leaving the brushstrokes visible. The overall appearance may be crude, but the overlapping layers play on effects of transparency, and there is a very subtle range of values in the colours.

"Painting remains to be done", Picasso said at the end of his life, as if everything had to be started all over again, as if painting were only in its infancy, at an archaic stage, just showing the results of its first awkward efforts.

After having overthrown, in his Cubist period, conventions inherited from the Renaissance (illusionistic perspective), Picasso created a new pictorial space and opened up new fields of exploration in painting. And at the end of "this frightening voyage", after having said it all and in every possible way, after having taken up again the burden of tradition and the legacy of his masters in the last years, after all this came an ultimate question that cast doubt on everything he had come to know: what is painting, and how does one paint?

101 Seated Old Man
Vieil homme assis

This flamboyant picture, which condenses into a single image a host of formal, pictorial and symbolic references, is the most poignant and tragic of Picasso's self-portraits. It is a portrait of the artist at the end of his life, but also that of Matisse, Van Gogh, Renoir and Cézanne all rolled into one. The dramatic representation of the painter on the threshold of death, "crumbling under the weight of knowledge and existence",[11] expresses solitude, and the "nostalgia and world-weariness"[12] of eyes that have seen everything and that, in the final moments, remember certain deeply-rooted images. It stands for the violent passion of painting, to which Renoir sacrificed his hand and Van Gogh his ear. But Picasso is still Picasso, and his vital energy, evinced in feverish brushstrokes, garish colours, pentimentos and smudges, transforms old age into an apotheosis.

"The Matisse sleeve that becomes the back of the armchair, the portrait of the stricken painter who mutilates himself, his hand becoming a stump,

Portrait of Auguste Renoir, (after the photograph), Musée Picasso, Paris

a sort of gardener with an old-fashioned sailor's beard sitting in a wicker chair against a background ablaze with colour, the old man who paints his tragic likeness with the lightly-sketched features of a child as a pretext to preserve the attributes of his art—the Van Gogh hat, the brush, the palette. Everything in this picture leads me to see it as the depiction of ultimate solitude, when all of the images seen and loved present themselves one last time to the memory, but without being able to render our features or tell our story, which is the story of the images we have loved and their catastrophic encounter."[13]

The most obvious reference in this painting is to Matisse: a drawing from 1971 shows a bearded old man with a hat bearing the inscription "*un peu Matisse*" ("somewhat Matisse"). There is also the warm contrast between the bright orange and cobalt blue, and an allusion to the *Women with a Peasant Blouse* (1940, Musée National d'Art Moderne, Paris) in the wing of the chair. All this indicates that we have here a last homage to the one whom Picasso called the "old white-haired and bearded god". The motif of the broad-brimmed straw hat

Photograph of Auguste Renoir, Picasso Archives

comes from Van Gogh's self-portraits, and may be seen in the related picture from 1972 called *The Young Painter* (Musée Picasso, Paris). The position of the seated old man has something of Cézanne's *Portrait of the Gardener Vallier* (1900-06, Tate Gallery, London), whose thoughtful wisdom was the fruit of a meditative and solitary existence.

Then there is the obscene stump of the amputated hand, the element that gives the figure its powerfulness and strangeness, and which is probably a reference to Renoir's paralysed hand. Picasso had a photograph of the aged Renoir that he once copied in a drawing. "The missing hand is here not a metaphor or a suggestion, but an erasure, an act of violence."[14] It has been effaced; what is left is like a thumb sticking out of a palette, seemingly attached to an arm composed of long streaks of blue paint.

The ultimate key to this painting would seem to be mutilation, an expression of the fear of death, of the painter's fear of being unable to paint, at one time suggested by blindness, now by dismemberment.

"It is moreover remarkable that, in this picture full of signs, it is perhaps the most obscure element that draws our attention the most. This stump should not be explained away; through it, Picasso will forever hold the ghastly pose of the 'man with the missing hand'."[15]

The Painter, 1971, Musée Reattu, Arles

The Young Painter, 1972, Musée Picasso, Paris ▷

101 *Seated Old Man*, 1970/71, Mougins. Oil on canvas, 145.5 x 114 cm ▷

102 Motherhood
Maternité

During the decade 1963–73 Picasso stripped his compositions down to the bare essentials, reducing his subject-matter to the nudes, the male figure, the couple, with, of course, the perennial theme of the woman represented in every possible position: sleeping, offering herself, fertile, relieving herself.

The theme of motherhood, a celebration of new life, often appears in Picasso's work and may be seen in the 1907 *Mother and Child* (pl. 8) and *The Woman with the Pushchair* from 1950 (pl. 86). At each period of his career, Picasso represented the theme in the specific pictorial idiom of the moment.

The 1971 *Motherhood*, which has a companion-piece in the *Man with Flute and Child*, shows the woman seated, holding the child in her arms. Both figures are contained in a figure-eight shape, and the eyes are enormous, as in all the faces of this period. The child, sitting with his legs apart, has an apple in his hand. His profile recalls those of ancient Greece; his eye, like the symbolic eye of ancient Egypt, has a diamond shape. The woman, who—like the child—has no neck, is represented in frontal and profile views, with her mouth contraposed to the nose. She wears a large hat (a frequently recurring motif in the last years) that both outlines and merges with the face. Colour and form fuse together. The violent black/white contrasts are attenuated by touches of pastel colours: pink, green and pale yellow.

Man with Flute and Child, 1971, private collection, Paris

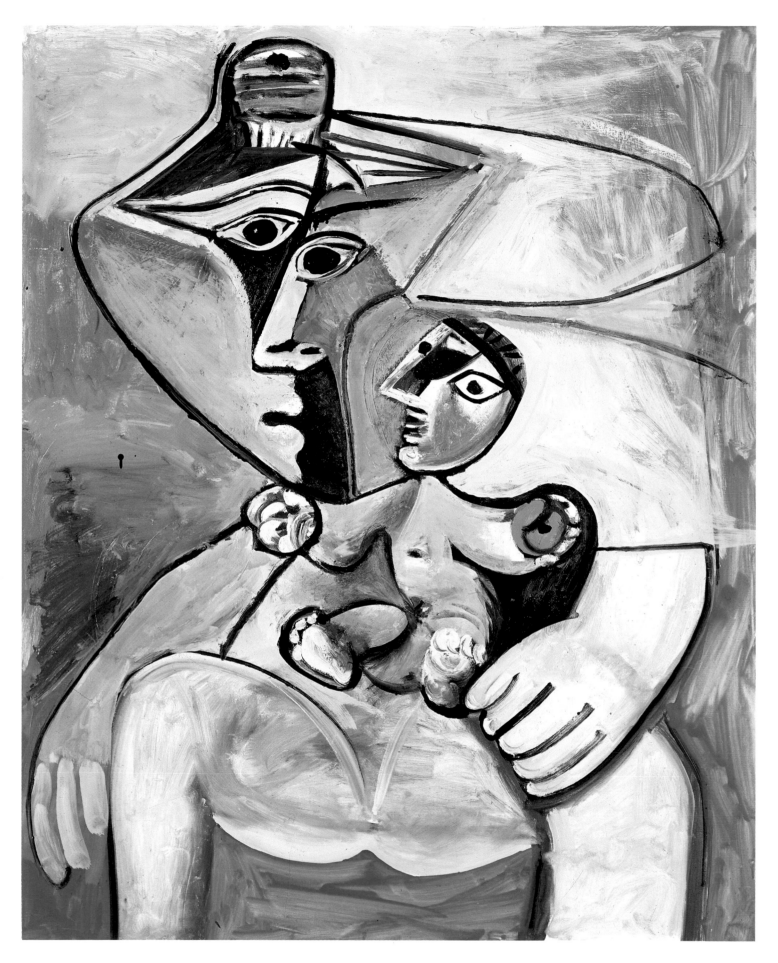

102 *Motherhood*, 30 August 1971, Mougins. Oil on canvas, 162 x 130 cm

103 Landscape
Paysage

Picasso, more drawn to the representation of the human figure, painted few landscapes, and those that he did paint are rarely "pure" landscapes. More often than not they are views of the surrounding countryside visible from his window, depicted in perspective or panoramic view. Picasso was more interested in the qualities or features of a specific landscape than in the genre itself; he was also more concerned with pictorial problems than with the expression of states of mind or feelings. Nature was not something to reflect upon, but rather an environment, a spectacle, and above all a matter of "forms". The house, trees and picturesque elements of his Mediterranean estate meant more to him than some uninhabited expanse of countryside. Nature was something to be domesticated, subjugated to his pictorial architecture. He contained it within black contours and tempered its exuberance with a network of thick lines. In this *Landscape* from Mougins, the last in this period of works as "dark as Golgotha",[16] only the forms of the hills and palm-trees help to identify the location; all of the other motifs are difficult to read.

Picasso painted this canvas in March 1972, at the age of 91, in the violent, energetic and sketchy manner characteristic of his late Avignon period. During this last phase he attained complete freedom—"free figuration"—and celebrated painting as an autonomous, living medium that creates its own forms. Brush-effects, impasto, running of colours, transparency of superimposed layers of paint, all contribute to the richness of texture. The vocabulary is emphatic: black and white spots, spirals, radiating stripes, zig-zags, fishbone patterns, a vertical line terminating in a circle, a downward-pointing arrow. All of these motifs are interwoven, creating a network of vectors that structures the composition, controls the dense paint medium and gives the impression of painting in the making. The dramatic effect is heightened by the greenish, opaque tonality of the whole. The pictorial motifs are like ideogrammes, and can be seen in other paintings: the fishbone pattern appears in a 1971 portrait,[17] in *The Musician* from 1972

(Musée Picasso, Paris), and associated with female genitals in two drawings.[18] The arrow and line with circle are also sexual symbols.

Picasso treated nature like the living organism that it is. Whether he painted a bouquet of flowers or a woman's body, he charged it with his own raw, elemental vitality.

At the moment of his "old age", he gave the supreme example of a return to the "infancy" of art.

The Musician, 1972, Musée Picasso, Paris

103 *Landscape*, 31 March 1972, Mougins. Oil on canvas, 130 x 162 cm

Notes

Introduction
1 Zervos 10: 37–42.
2 Zervos 10: 37–42.
3 *Catalogue sommaire du Musée Picasso*, vol. 1.
4 José Bergamin, *Picasso Laureatus*. Denoël, Paris 1985, p. 11.

The Hôtel Salé
1 In *Musées et Monuments Historiques*, no. 104, Sept. 1979, pp. 42–48.

The Blue Period
1 Zervos 1: 52; 21: 177, 178, 179.
2 Zervos 1: 55.
3 Charles Morice, in *Mercure de France*, Paris, December 1902.
4 Quoted in Leymarie, p. 2.
5 Carl G. Jung, in *Neue Zürcher Zeitung*, 13 November 1932.
6 Alberto Moravia, "Explosion de la manière", in *Tout l'œuvre peint de Picasso: périodes bleue et rose*. Flammarion, Paris 1980.

The Rose Period
1 Olivier, p. 135.
2 Daix and Boudaille 15: 3–6.
3 Zervos 1: 360.
4 Alfred H. Barr, *Picasso, Fifty Years of His Art*, exhibition catalogue. The Museum of Modern Art, New York 1946, p. 46.
5 Françoise Gilot, "Picasso, peintre de chevalet", in *L'année de la peinture*. Calmann Lévy, Paris 1980, p. 183.

The Demoiselles Period
1 In 1907, Picasso bought an Iberian sculpture from Géry-Piéret without knowing that this *Male Head* had been stolen from the Louvre.
2 Seckel 1988, 1: 46.
3 Leo Steinberg, in Seckel 1988, 2: 348.

Cubism
1 Seckel 1985, p. 28.
2 Zervos 28: 48.
3 Zervos 28: 84, 85, 89, 99.
4 Zervos 28: 237.

Collages
1 I. Monod-Fontaine, *Georges Braque, Les Papiers collés*, exhibition catalogue. Musée National d'Art Moderne, Paris 1982.

2 Daix and Rosselet, pp. 664–70.
3 Werner Spies, *Les sculptures de Picasso*. Clairefontaine, Lausanne 1971, p. 48.

Return to Representation
1, 2 Pierre Daix, *Picasso, la Provence et Jacqueline*. Espace Van Gogh, Arles 1991, p. 78.
3 Zervos 3: 233.
4 Pierre de Champris, *Picasso, ombre et soleil*. Gallimard, Paris 1960, p. 90.

The Neoclassical Period
1 Jean Cocteau, *Picasso*. Stock, Paris 1923.
2 Dominique Bozo, preface to *Picasso: Œuvres reçues*.
3 T. Reff, "Picasso's Three Musicians: Masters, Artists and Friends". *Art in America*, Dec. 1980.
4 The hat could also be Apollinaire's (see the 1902 photograph in P.M. Adema, *Guillaume Apollinaire*, Table Ronde, Paris 1968).
5 Zervos 2: 84.
6 "I want to show you great paintings like Poussin's", the poet wrote to Picasso in 1918 (archives of the Picasso Museum).
7 Marie-Laure Bernadac, *Picasso et la Méditerranée*, exhibition catalogue. Villa Médici, Rome 1982/83, p. 121.
8 Daix 1977, p. 181.
9 Zervos 5: 173, 174.
10 Zervos 5: 176.
11 Leymarie, p. 5.
12 Pierre Reverdy, *Les Peintres français nouveaux*, Paris 1924, p. 114.
13 Fermigier, p. 161.

On the Fringes of Surrealism I
1 Zervos 5: 460.
2 *Picasso*, exhibition catalogue. Rome/Milan 1953.
3 Robert Rosenblum, *Picassos from the Musée Picasso, Paris*, exhibition catalogue. Walker Art Center, Minneapolis 1980.
4 Georges Bataille, *Manet*. Skira, Paris 1955.
5 Penrose 1958, p. 232.
6 Lydia Gasman, *Mystery, Magic and Love in Picasso, 1925–1937*, doctoral thesis.

Columbia University, New York 1981.
7 Carlton Lake, "Picasso speaking". *The Atlantic Monthly*, July 1957.
8 *Les Quatre Petites Filles* (1947-48). Gallimand, Paris 1969. *Poèmes, lithographies.* Louis Carré et Maximilien Vox, Paris 1949. "Poème" (1935), in Sabartés 1946.
9 Quoted in *Donation Louise et Michel Leiris, Collection Kahnweiler-Leiris*, exhibition catalogue. Musée National d'Art Moderne, Paris 1984, p. 168.
10 The monogram appears in several pictures (Zervos 7: 55, 58, 110), and Picasso sometimes added his own initial, "MTP" (Zervos 7: 54).
11 See Zervos 7: 10, in which the body of the guitar looks like a decorated pillowcase.

The Bathers
1 Dominique Bozo, in *Picasso: Œuvres reçues*.
2, 3 Christian Zervos, "Picasso à Dinard". *Cahiers d'Art* 1929, pp. 5-6.
4 Michel Leiris, "Toiles récentes de Picasso". *Documents* 2/2, 1930, p. 70.
5 Guillaume Apollinaire, *Le poète assassiné*, 1916.

On the Fringes of Surrealism II
1 See *Guitar* (pl. 33).
2, 3, 4 Fermigier, p. 201.
5 Zervos 7: 347.
6 André Breton, "Picasso dans son élément." *Minotaure* 1, 1933, p. 16.
7 Zervos 7: 311.
8 Ruth Kaufmann, "Picasso's *Crucifixion* of 1930". *The Burlington Magazine*, September 1969.
9 Zervos 7: 315.
10 Fermigier, p. 262.
11 André Breton, *Le Surréalisme et la peinture*. Gallimard, Paris 1965, p. 56.
12 Quoted by D. Bozo in *Picasso: Œuvres reçues*, p. 121.
13 André Breton, "Picasso dans son élément". *Minotaure* 1, 1933.
14 Raynal, p. 58.
15 Pierre Reverdy (1918), quoted in Pierre Daix,

Picasso. Somogy, Paris 1964, p. 144.

Boisgeloup and Marie-Thérèse
1 Bloch, no. 282.
2 Brassaï, p. 28.
3 Leymarie, p. 53.
4 Malraux, p. 129.
5 Werner Spies, *Les Sculptures de Picasso*. Clairefontaine, Lausanne 1971, p. 141.

Portraits
1, 2 Dominique Bozo, "Le modèle en question, sur quelques portraits 1930–1940." *Le Courrier de l'Unesco*, December 1980.
3 Brassaï, p. 64.
4 Daix 1977, p. 278.
5 With the artist's approval, and at the suggestion of André Malraux, two black-and-white and two colour versions of the design were woven at the Manufactures Nationales des Gobelins.
6 Brassaï, p. 58.
7 Dominique Bozo, in *Picasso: Œuvres reçues*.

The War Years
1 Vallentin, p. 332.
2 D.-H. Kahnweiler, *Les Sculptures de Picasso*. Du Chêne, Paris 1948, unpaginated.
3 Picasso, "Permanence du sacré". *XXe Siècle* 24, December 1954.
4 Brassaï, p. 90.
5 See note 2.
6 Malraux, p. 34. "The scythe evidently suggests death, which is why an enlargement of this figure seemed so appropriate for Baudelaire", p. 40.
7 Brassaï, p. 98.
8, 9 Malraux, p. 40.
10 Malraux, p. 36.

Still-Lifes and Vanitas
1 Vallentin, p. 369.
2, 3 Gilot and Lake, p. 280.
4 Zervos 16: 199, 200, 298.
5 Werner Spies, *Les Sculptures de Picasso*. Clairefontaine, Lausanne 1971, p. 180.

Sculpture and Assemblage
1 Duncan 1974, p. 7.
2 Odysseus Elytis, "Équivalences chez Picasso". *Verve* 7 (25, 26).

3 Malraux, p. 32.
4 Gilot and Lake, p. 290.

The Fifties
1 Zervos 16: 97.
2 Duncan (1961, p. 180) has interpreted this motif as the branches of a Christmas tree.
3 Bernadac 1988, p. 20.
4 Zervos 16: 96.
5 See note 3.
6 Duncan 1961, p. 183.
7 Zervos 16: 325.
8 Zervos 16: 327–30.
9 Zervos 16: 331.
10 Zervos 16: 427–29, 449–51, 453–55, 457–71.
11 Daix 1977, p. 362.
12 Spies and Piot, pp. 543, 559, 548.
13 Daix 1977, pp. 372–73.
14 Zervos 18: 91, 93.
15 Zervos 18: 95–98.
16 Daix 1977, p. 376.

The Last Years
1 Picasso Archives, Musée Picasso.
2 Douglas Cooper, *Les Déjeuners*. Cercle d'Art, Paris 1962.
3 Picasso to Gonzalez, in Dore Ashton, *Picasso on Art*. Viking Press, New York 1972.
4 Bernadac 1988, p. 43.
5 Zervos 33: 148.
6 Zervos 31: 309, 310.
7 Zervos 31: 311, 312.
8 Hélène Parmelin, *Le Peintre et son modèle*. Cercle d'Art, Paris 1965, p. 80.
9 The exhibition of the *dation* at the Grand-Palais in Paris in 1979/80 may have had the same impact on the art world as the Cézanne retrospective in 1907. Other international exhibitions have confirmed this reappraisal: Pace Gallery, New York (1981), Kunstmuseum, Basle (1981), Guggenheim Museum, New York (1983).
10 In both cases there was a ten-year delay before the work received proper recognition.
11-15 Jean-Michel Michelena, *Vieil homme au chapeau assis*. C.A.P.C., Bordeaux 1983.
16 Dominique Bozo, in *Picasso: Œuvres reçues*.
17 Zervos 33: 397.
18 Zervos 33: 470, 499.

Picasso (photo by E. Quinn)

Biography

1881
25 October, Málaga: birth of Pablo, the first child of José Ruiz Blasco and María Picasso y López.

1891
September: the Ruiz family moves to La Coruña.

1895
José Ruiz appointed professor at La Lonja, the school of fine arts in Barcelona.
Summer: Pablo visits Madrid and Barcelona. Spends summer in Málaga and returns to Barcelona by sea. Paints seascapes during the trip.
Winter: first large academic picture, *The First Communion* (Museu Picasso, Barcelona).

1896
Spends summer vacation in Málaga, paints landscapes and bullfights.

1897
Science and Charity (Museu Picasso, Barcelona).
September: leaves for Madrid.
October: passes the entrance examination to the Academia San Fernando with excellent results.

1898
June: returns to Barcelona, then leaves for Horta, the native village of his friend Pallarés, south of the Ebro, near Gandesa.

1899
February: returns to Barcelona. Joins the Els Quatre Gats circle and meets Jaime Sabartés and Casagemas.

1900
1 February: exhibits at Els Quatre Gats.
October: leaves for Paris with Casagemas. Works in Nonell's studio in Montmartre. Meets the businessman Pere Manyach and the art-dealer Berthe Weill; sells several pastels.
20 December: returns to Barcelona with Casagemas, whom he also takes to Málaga.

1901
Leaves for Madrid.
17 February: Casagemas commits suicide in Paris.
April: returns to Barcelona.
May: leaves for Paris and establishes himself at 130 ter, boulevard de Clichy, in Casagemas's former studio.
25 June–14 July: Picasso and Itturrino exhibit at the Vollard gallery in Paris. Meets the poet Max Jacob.
Winter: *Self-Portrait* in blue (Musée Picasso, Paris).

1902
Late January: returns to Barcelona.
1–15 April: Picasso and Lemaire exhibit at the Berthe Weill gallery.
October: returns to Paris with Sebastian Junyer.
15 November–15 December: group exhibition at Berthe Weill's (Blue Period works).

1903
January: returns to Barcelona.
Spring: begins *Life* (The Cleveland Museum of Art).

1904
April: leaves for Paris, establishes himself at the Bateau-Lavoir in Paco Durio's former studio.

The Bateau-Lavoir around 1904. Picasso has marked the location of his studio (Picasso Archives)

Autumn: Rose Period paintings on the theme of motherhood. Meets Apollinaire and André Salmon.
Meets Fernande Olivier.

1905
25 February–6 March: exhibits his first Rose Period paintings at the Serrurier Gallery.
Spring: *The Mountebanks* (National Gallery of Art, Washington, D.C.).
Summer: trip to Schoorl, Holland, where he paints *Three Dutch Girls* (Musée National d'Art Moderne, Paris, on permanent loan to Musée Picasso).
Autumn: meets Gertrude and Leo Stein. Theme of the death of Harlequin.

Picasso and Fernande Olivier in Montmartre, c. 1906 (Picasso Archives)

1906
Gertrude Stein introduces Picasso to Matisse.
Early March: Vollard buys most of the Rose Period paintings.

Early May: leaves for Barcelona with Fernande.

Mid-May: leaves with Fernande for Gósol, a remote village in Upper Catalonia; theme of the two brothers.

Finishes his *Portrait of Gertrude Stein* (The Metropolitan Museum of Art, New York), begun in the winter of 1905.

1907

Begins work on *The Young Ladies of Avignon* (*Les Demoiselles d'Avignon*, The Museum of Modern Art, New York).

Late May: finishes first state of *Les Demoiselles*.

Early July: final state of *Les Demoiselles*.

Early summer: Kahnweiler's first visit to the Bateau-Lavoir.

Late September: Braque visits Picasso.

1 October: Cézanne retrospective at the Salon d'Automne.

1908

Friendship (Hermitage Museum, St. Petersburg). *Standing Nude* (Museum of Fine Arts, Boston).

August: sojourn at La Rue-des-Bois, a village 60 km north of Paris.

October: final version of *Three Women* (Hermitage Museum, St. Petersburg).

1909

May: leaves for Barcelona. Goes to Horta de Ebro with Fernande, paints landscapes (The Museum of Modern Art, New York).

The studio at Horta de Ebro, 1909 (Picasso Archives)

September: returns to Paris and moves to 11, boulevard de Clichy.

Autumn: sculpture *Head of Fernande* (Musée Picasso, Paris).

1910

Portraits of *Ambroise Vollard* (Pushkin Museum, Moscow) and *Wilhelm Uhde* (Pulitzer Collection, St. Louis).

Late June: leaves with Fernande for Barcelona, then goes to Cadaqués.

Autumn: *Portrait of Kahnweiler* (The Art Institute of Chicago).

Picasso in the Boulevard de Clichy studio, c. 1910 (Picasso Archives)

1911

July: leaves for Céret, a village in French Catalonia; Braque and Fernande join him there in August.

Marie Laurencin photographed by Picasso in the Boulevard de Clichy studio, 1911 (Picasso Archives)

Braque in military uniform photographed by Picasso in the Boulevard de Clichy studio, 1911 (Picasso Archives)

5 September: returns to Paris.

1 October: Cubist room at the Salon d'Automne, but Picasso does not exhibit.

Autumn: meets Éva Gouel, "Ma Jolie".

Picasso in his studio at the Bateau-Lavoir, 1908 (photo by Gelett Burgess, Picasso Archives)

1912

Spring: first collage, *Still-Life with Wicker-work Chair* (Musée Picasso, Paris).
First assemblages: "Guitars" made of cardboard (Musée Picasso, Paris) and metal (The Museum of Modern Art, New York).

Eva Gouel (Marcelle Humbert), 1911/12 (Picasso Archives)

The wall of the studio at 242, Boulevard de Raspail, November/December 1912

18 May: leaves for Céret with Éva.
21 June: leaves Céret for Avignon.
25 June: moves to Sorgues, a village north of Avignon.
July: Braque arrives with his wife.
Mid-September: Braque makes his first *papier collé* while Picasso is away in Paris.
October: returns from Sorgues and moves to 242, boulevard Raspail.
November: makes his first *papiers collés* and paints pictures derived from them.
18 December: contract between Picasso and Kahnweiler.

1913

March: leaves for Céret with Éva.
September: moves to Rue Schoelcher.

1914

Spring: *Glass of Absinth*.
June: leaves for Avignon.
July: returns to portraiture.

1915

14 December: death of Éva Gouel.

1916

May: Cocteau introduces Diaghilev to Picasso.
Summer: in Montrouge, a southern suburb of Paris.
August: agrees to collaborate on *Parade* (music by Erik Satie).

Girl with Bare Feet, 1895, in the Rue Schoelcher studio, 1914 (Picasso Archives)

Picasso in the Rue Schoelcher studio, c. 1915 (Picasso Archives)

1917

Paris: works on *Parade*.
17 February: leaves for Rome with Cocteau.
Early February: takes apartment in Via Margutta in Rome, near the Villa Medici. Draws many portraits, paints *The Italian Woman*, *Harlequin* and *Woman with a Necklace*.

Olga, Picasso and Cocteau in Rome, 1917
(Archives, Musée Picasso)

Meets Olga Koklova and Stravinsky.
Late March: trip to Naples and Pompeii.
Late April: returns to Paris.
18 May: first performance of *Parade* at the
Théâtre du Châtelet.
Early June: leaves for Madrid with
Diaghilev's troupe and Olga.
12 July: banquet given in his honour at Bar-
celona.
Late November: Olga and Picasso live in
Montrouge.

Picasso and the painters of the stage-curtain for
Parade, Rome, 1917 (Picasso Archives)

1918
23 January–15 February: Matisse/Picasso
exhibition at Paul Guillaume's gallery.
12 July: Picasso and Olga marry at the Russian Church in Paris, with Cocteau, Max
Jacob and Apollinaire acting as witnesses.
Sojourn in Biarritz. Paints *The Bathers* (Musée
Picasso, Paris).
Late November: moves to 44, rue La Boétie.

Olga and Picasso in the London studio where the
stage-curtain for *The Three-Cornered Hat* was
made, London, 1919 (Picasso Archives)

1919
Early May: leaves for London to work on the
ballet *The Three-Cornered Hat*, with music
by Manuel de Falla.
Summer: sojourns at Biarritz with Mme. Fr-
razuriz, then goes to Saint-Raphael (Côte
d'Azur) with Olga.

1920
15 May: first performance of *Pulcinella*, with
music by Stravinsky.
June: leaves with Olga for Juan-les-Pins
(Côte d'Azur).

1921
4 February: birth of Paulo.
22 May: first performance of *Flamenco
Scene* (traditional Andalusian music adapted
by Manuel de Falla).
Summer: moves with Olga and Paulo to Fon-
tainebleau, where he paints *Three Women at
the Fountain* (Musée Picasso, Paris and The
Museum of Modern Art, New York), and *The
Three Musicians* (The Museum of Modern
Art, New York and Philadelphia Museum of
Art).

1922
June: summers at Dinard (Brittany coast).
Paints *Two Women Running on the Beach*
(Musée Picasso, Paris).

December: designs stage set for Cocteau's *Antigone*, produced by Charles Dullin at the Théâtre de l'Atelier.

1923

Summer: vacations at Cap d'Antibes (Côte d'Azur). Paints *The Pipes of Pan* (Musée Picasso, Paris) during the summer.

1924

18 June: first performance of *Mercury* with music by Satie.
20 June: first performance of *The Blue Train* with music by Darius Milhaud.
Summer: stays at Juan-les-Pins (Côte d'Azur), in Villa La Vigie. Sketchbook with abstract drawings.
Paints *Paulo as Harlequin* (Musée Picasso, Paris).

1925

March–April: in Monte Carlo.
June–July: finishes *The Dance* (Tate Gallery, London).
July: spends holiday at Juan-les-Pins, paints *The Kiss* (Musée Picasso, Paris).
14 November: participates in the first exhibition of the Surrealists at the Pierre gallery.

1926

The Painter and His Model (Musée Picasso, Paris).
Spring: *Guitar* with nails (Musée Picasso, Paris). Summers at Juan-les-Pins.
October: trip to Barcelona.

1927

January: meets Marie-Thérèse Walter.
Summer: spends holiday at Cannes.

1928

January: executes the large collage *Minotaur* (Musée National d'Art Moderne, Paris).
Autumn: works on metal sculptures with Julio González.

1929

Spring: *The Woman in the Garden* (Musée Picasso, Paris).
Summer: last sojourn at Dinard.
Large Nude in a Red Armchair (Musée Picasso, Paris).

1930

February: *The Crucifixion*.
June: buys the Château de Boisgeloup, near Gisors, 80 km northwest of Paris.
Summers at Juan-les-Pins.
Autumn: Marie-Thérèse moves to 44, rue La Boétie.

Picasso in his sculpture studio at Boisgeloup, 1931 (Photo by Bernès-Marouteau)

1931

January: *Figures on the Seashore* (Musée Picasso, Paris).
March: *Large Still-Life with Pedestal Table* (Musée Picasso, Paris).
May: first stay at Boisgeloup.
Summer: holiday at Juan-les-Pins.
Publication of two important illustrated books, Ovid's *Metamorphoses* (Skira, Lausanne) and Balzac's *Unknown Masterpiece* (Ambroise Vollard, Paris).

Tériade and a dog at the door of the Boisgeloup studio, 1932 (photo by Brassaï)

1932

Girl in Front of the Mirror (The Museum of Modern Art, New York).
June: retrospectives at the Georges Petit gallery and at the Kunsthaus in Zurich.
Summer: works on sculpted heads after Marie-Thérèse at Boisgeloup.
Series of drawings on *The Crucifixion* after Grünewald.

1933

25 May: first issue of *Minotaure*, with cover by Picasso.
Summer: spends holiday at Cannes with Olga and Paulo.
Mid-August: leaves for Barcelona and stays until the end of the month.
September: paints *Corrida: The Death of the Torero* at Boisgeloup (Musée Picasso, Paris).

Dummy of the cover for the first issue of *Minotaure*, Paris, 1933 (Museum of Modern Art, New York)

1934

June–September: series of paintings, drawings and etchings on the theme of the bullfight.
Late August: travels in Spain with Olga and Paulo.
Attends bullfights in Burgos and Madrid. Visits the Museum of Catalonian Art in Barcelona.
Series of sculptures with cast textures: *Woman with Foliage, The Woman with the Orange* (Musée Picasso, Paris).

1935

Spring: exhibition of *papiers collés* at the Galerie Pierre.

Minotauromachy etchings.
June: separation from Olga.
5 September: Marie-Thérèse gives birth to Maya.

1936
25 March: Picasso leaves secretly for Juan-les-Pins with Marie-Thérèse and Maya.
Gouaches and drawings on the theme of the Minotaur.
Appointed director of the Prado.
Early August: Picasso leaves for Mougins, joined by Dora Maar.
Autumn: Picasso works in a studio at Le Tremblay-sur-Mauldre (northwest of Paris, near Montfort-l'Amaury) lent by Ambroise Vollard. Marie-Thérèse and Maya reside there until 1940.

Picasso painting *Guernica* in the Rue des Grands-Augustins studio, 1937 (photo by Dora Maar)

1937
Winter: Picasso rents a studio at 7, rue des Grands-Augustins.
February–early March: works at Le Tremblay-sur-Mauldre.
26 April: bombing of Guernica.
Mid-June: finishes *Guernica*, which is exhibited in the Spanish pavilion at the Paris International Exhibition.
October–December: *The Weeping Woman* (Musée Picasso, Paris and Tate Gallery, London).

1938
Large collage, *Women at Their Toilette* (Musée Picasso, Paris).
July: leaves for Mougins with Dora Maar.

Picasso in the Rue des Grands-Augustins studio, 1938 (photo by Peter Rose Pulham)

The performers of *Desire Caught by the Tail* in Picasso's home, 16 June 1944 (photo by Brassaï)

1939
Early July: leaves with Dora Maar to stay with Man Ray in Antibes.
Night Fishing at Antibes (The Museum of Modern Art, New York).
1 September: leaves for Royan.
Series of "Women with Hats".

1940
Spends beginning of the year at Royan.

1941
Writes his first surrealistic play, *Desire Caught by the Tail* (*Le Désir attrapé par la queue*), published in 1944.

1942
Spring: assemblage *Bull's Head* (Musée Picasso, Paris).
4 May: finishes *The Aubade* (Musée National d'Art Moderne, Paris).

1943
February–March: executes *The Man with the Sheep* (Musée Picasso, Paris).
May: meets Françoise Gilot.

1944
19 March: private performance of *Desire Caught by the Tail*.
Mid-August: stays at Marie-Thérèse's apartment during the liberation of Paris.
5 October: joins French Communist Party.
7 October: opening of the Salon d'Automne and the Picasso retrospective.

1945

April–May: *The Charnel-House* (The Museum of Modern Art, New York).
July: leaves with Dora Maar for Cap d'Antibes.
26 November: reunited with Françoise.

1946

Mid-March: Picasso joins Françoise at Golfe-Juan.
Visits Matisse in Nice.
Early July: Françoise and Picasso leave for Ménerbes (Vaucluse).
Early August: moves to Louis Fort's home in Golfe-Juan.
October: begins decorating the Palais Grimaldi at Antibes.
First trip to Vallauris.

1947

15 May: birth of Claude.
June: departure for Golfe-Juan.
August: begins working in ceramics.
Writes second play, *The Four Little Girls* (*Les quatre petites filles*).

1948

25 August: attends the Congress of Intellectuals for Peace in Wroclaw, Poland.
Mid-September: returns to Vallauris.
Paints two versions of *The Kitchen* (Musée Picasso, Paris and The Museum of Modern Art, New York).

Picasso at Madoura's using a light-pencil, 1949 (photo by Gjon Mili)

Picasso, Françoise Gilot, Claude and Paloma at Vallauris, 1952/53 (photo by Edward Quinn)

19 April: birth of Paloma.
Spring: returns to Vallauris and buys the Le Fournas workshops.

1950

6 August: Laurent Casanova unveils *The Man with the Sheep* at Vallauris.
Sculptures *The Goat, The Woman with the Pushchair, Little Girl Skipping* (Musée Picasso, Paris).

1951

15 January: *Massacre in Korea* (Musée Picasso, Paris).

1952

Drawings for the *War and Peace* murals to decorate the chapel of Vallauris.

1953

March: Picasso's *Portrait of Stalin* printed in *Lettres Françaises* causes a scandal.
Françoise leaves with the children for Paris.

1954

April: portraits of Sylvette David.
June: meets Jacqueline Roque.
December: begins series of variations based on Delacroix's *Women of Algiers*.

Picasso working in his studio at Vallauris, 1948

Massacre in Korea, Vallauris, 1951 (Musée Picasso)

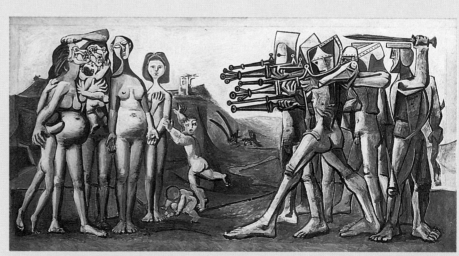

1949

February: Aragon chooses Picasso's *Dove* for the poster of the Peace Congress that opens in Paris on 20 April.

The goat at La Californie, 1955 (photo by David Douglas Duncan)

Picasso and Jacqueline at La Californie (photo by Man Ray)

Picasso in front of *The Fall of Icarus*, 1958 (photo by Edward Quinn)

1955
May: leaves Paris with Jacqueline for the Midi. Moves into the villa La Californie in Cannes.
June: retrospective at the Musée des Arts Décoratifs in Paris.

The filming of Henri-Georges Clouzot's *Mystery of Picasso*, 1955 (photo by Edward Quinn)

Summer: works with Henri-Georges Clouzot on the film *The Mystery of Picasso* (*Le Mystère Picasso*).

1956
The wood sculptures *The Bathers* (Staatsgalerie, Stuttgart) are cast in bronze (Musée Picasso, Paris).
Paints *The Studio at La Californie* (Musée Picasso, Paris).

Jacqueline, Picasso and Jean Cocteau, with Paloma, Maya and Claude in the background, watching a bullfight, Vallauris, 1955 (photo by Brian Brake)

1957
17 August: begins work on *Las Meninas* (Museu Picasso, Barcelona).

1958
29 March: unveiling of the mural *The Fall of Icarus* at UNESCO headquarters in Paris.
September: buys the Château de Vauvenargues.

The Château de Vauvenargues, postcard (Musée Picasso)

Picasso at the Mas Notre-Dame-de-Vie, Mougins, c. 1965 (photo by A. Gomes, Musée Picasso) ▷

Paints *The Bay of Cannes* (Musée Picasso, Paris).

1959
10 August: first drawings of *The Luncheon on the Grass* (*Le Déjeuner sur l'herbe*) after Manet.

1961
2 March: marries Jacqueline Roque in Vallauris.
June: moves to the farmhouse Notre-Dame-de-Vie in Mougins, near Cannes.
Works on painted sheet metal sculptures: *Chair, Woman with Outstretched Arms, Woman and Child, Footballers* (Musée Picasso, Paris).

1962
November: *The Rape of the Sabines* (one version at the Musée National d'Art Moderne in Paris).

1966
19 November: opening of the retrospective at the Grand Palais and Petit Palais in Paris.

1967
Spring: Picasso evicted from his studio in the Rue des Grands-Augustins.

1970
January: donation of works in his family's collection to the Picasso museum in Barcelona.
May–October: exhibition at the Palais des Papes in Avignon.

1971
April: exhibition at the Louise Leiris Gallery of 194 drawings done between 15 December 1969 and 12 January 1971.

1973
January: exhibition at the Louise Leiris Gallery of 156 prints done between late 1970 and March 1972.
8 April: death of Picasso in Mougins.
May–September: exhibition of 201 paintings at the Palais des Papes in Avignon.

Select Bibliography

Reminiscences

Brassaï, *Conversations avec Picasso*, Paris, Gallimard, 1964. (English trans.: *Picasso and Company*, Garden City, N.Y., Doubleday, 1966, and London, Thames and Hudson, 1967).

Duncan, Douglas, *The Private World of Pablo Picasso*, Harper, New York and London, 1961.

——, *Goodbye Picasso*, Grosset & Dunlap, New York, 1974.

——, *The Silent Studio*, Norton, New York, and Collins, London, 1976.

——, *Viva Picasso: A Centennial Celebration 1881-1981*, Viking Press, New York, 1980.

Eluard, Paul, *A Pablo Picasso*, Les Trois Collines, Geneva, 1944. (English trans.: *Pablo Picasso*, Philosophical Library, New York, 1947).

Gilot, Françoise, and Carlton Lake, *Vivre avec Picasso*, Calmann-Lévy, Paris, 1965. (English trans.: *Life with Picasso*, Penguin, Harmondsworth, Middx, 1966).

Kahnweiler, Daniel-Henry, *Mes galeries et mes peintres, Entretiens avec Francis Crémieux*, Gallimard, Paris, 1961. (English trans.: *My Galleries and Painters*, Viking Press, New York, and Thames and Hudson, London, 1971).

——, *Confessions esthétiques*, Gallimard, Paris 1963.

Laporte, Geneviève, *"Si tard le soir, le soleil brille" Pablo Picasso*, Plon, Paris, 1973. (English trans.: *Sunshine at Midnight: Memories of Picasso and Cocteau*, Macmillan, New York, 1975, and Weidenfeld & Nicolson, London, 1975).

Malraux, André, *La tête d'obsidienne*, Gallimard, Paris, 1974. (English trans.: *Picasso's Mask*, Holt, Rinehart and Winston, New York, 1976).

Mili, Gjon, *Picasso et al troisième dimension*, Edition Triton, Paris, 1970. (English trans.: *Picasso's Third Dimension*, Triton Press, New York, 1970).

Olivier, Fernande, *Picasso et ses amis*, Stock, Paris, 1933. (English trans.: *Picasso and his Friends*, Appleton-Century-Crofts, New York, 1965).

Parmelin, Hélène, *Picasso sur la place*, Julliard, Paris, 1960. (English trans.: *Picasso Plain: an Intimate Portrait*, St. Martin's Press, New York, 1963, and Secker and Warburg, London, 1963).

——, *Picasso dit...*, Gonthier, Paris, 1966. (English trans.: *Picasso says...*, A. S. Barnes, South Brunswick, N.J., 1969, and Allen and Unwin, London, 1969).

——, *Voyage en Picasso*, Robert Laffont, Paris, 1980.

Penrose, Roland, *Portrait of Picasso*, 2nd ed., Lund Humphries, London, 1971, and Museum of Modern Art, New York, 1971.

Sabartés, Jaime, *Portraits et souvenirs*, Louis Carré et Maximilien Vox, Paris, 1946.

——, *Picasso: Documents iconographiques*, Pierre Cailler, Geneva, 1954.

Monographs

Berger, John *The Success and Failure of Picasso*, Penguin, Harmondsworth, Middx, 1966.

Bernadac, Marie-Laure, and Paule Du Bouchet, *Picasso le sage et le fou*, Gallimard, Paris, 1986.

Cabanne, Pierre, *Le siècle de Picasso*, 2 vols, Denoël, Paris, 1975.

Daix, Pierre, *La vie de peintre de Pablo Picasso*, Éditions du Seuil, Paris, 1977.

——, *Picasso Créateur*, Éditions du Seuil, Paris, 1987.

Fermigier, André, *Picasso*, Livre de Poche, Paris, 1969.

Giraudy, Danièle, *Picasso: La mémoire du regard*, Cercle d'Art, Paris, 1986.

Leymarie, Jean, *Picasso, Métamorphoses et Unité*, Geneva, Skira, 1971 (English trans.: *Picasso: The Artist of the Century*, London, MacMillan, 1972, and New York, Rizzoli, 1976).

Penrose, Roland, *Picasso: His Life and Work*, London, Victor Gollancz Ltd., 1958; repr. Penguin, Harmondsworth, Middx, 1971, and Harper, New York, 1973.

——, *Picasso 1881–1973*, Paul Elek, London, 1973.

Raynal, Maurice, *Picasso*, Skira, Geneva, 1953.

Richardson, John, *A Life of Picasso*, vol. 1: 1881–1906, New York, Random House, 1991.

Schiff, Gert (ed.), *Picasso in Perspective*, Englewood Cliffs, Prentice-Hall, 1976.

Stein, Gertrude, *Picasso*, Batsford, London, 1938, and Scribner, New York, 1939; repr. Dover Publications, Dover 1984.

Vallentin, Antonina. *Pablo Picasso*, Michel, Paris, 1957. (English trans.: *Picasso*, Doubleday, Garden City, N.Y., and Cassell, London, 1963).

Works of Reference

Baer, Brigitte, *Picasso peintre graveur*, 4 vols, Kornfeld, Berne, 1986–90.

Bernadac, Marie-Laure, and Christine Piot, *Picasso Ecrits*, Réunion des Musées Nationaux and Gallimard, Paris, 1989.

Bloch, Georges, *Pablo Picasso: Catalogue de l'œuvre gravé et lithographié*, 4 vols, Kornfeld and Klipstein, Berne, 1968–79.

Daix, Pierre, and Georges Boudaille, *Picasso, 1900–1906, catalogue raisonné de l'œuvre peint*. Ides et Calendes, Neuchâtel, 1966. (English trans.: *Picasso: The Blue and Rose Periods – A Catalogue Raisonné of the Paintings, 1900–1906*, New York Graphic Society, Greenwich, Conn., and Evelyn Adams and Mackay, London, 1967).

Daix, Pierre, and Joan Rosselet (ed.), *Le cubisme de Picasso, catalogue raisonné de l'œuvre peint*, Ides et Calendes, Neuchâtel, 1979. (Engl. trans.: *Picasso: The Cubist Years, 1907–1916 – A Catalogue Raisonné of the Paintings and Related Works*, Thames and Hudson, London, 1979).

Duncan, David Douglas, *Picasso's Picassos: The Treasures of La Californie*, Harper, New York, and Macmillan, London, 1961.

Geiser, Bernhard, *Picasso peintre-graveur*, 2 vols, Berne, published by the author, 1933, and Kornfeld und Klipstein, Berne, 1968.

Goeppert, Sebastian, Herma Goeppert-Frank and Patrick Cramer, *Pablo Picasso: Catalogue raisonné des livres illustrés*, Patrick Cramer, Geneva, 1983.

Mourlot, Fernand, *Picasso lithographe*, 4 vols, André Sauret, Monte Carlo, 1949–64.

Palau i Fabre, Josep, *Picasso vivant (1881–1907)*, Albin Michel, Paris, 1981.

——, *Picasso cubisme, 1907–1917*, Albin Michel, Paris, 1981.

Ramié, Georges, *Céramique de Picasso*, Cercle d'Art, Paris, 1974. (English trans.: *Picasso's Ceramics*, Viking Press, New York, 1976).

Spies, Werner, *Sculpture by Picasso*, Abrams, New York, 1971. (Also published as *Picasso Sculpture*, Thames and Hudson, London, 1972).

Zervos, Christian, *Pablo Picasso*, 33 vols, Éditions Cahiers d'Art, Paris, 1932–78.

Exhibition Catalogues

Bernadac, Marie-Laure, *Le dernier Picasso*, Musée National d'Art Moderne, Paris, 1988.

Pablo Picasso: A Restrospective, The Museum of Modern Art, New York, 1980.

Picasso: Œuvres reçues en paiement des droits de succession, Grand Palais, Paris, 1979/80.

Rubin, William, *Picasso – Braque: Pioneering Cubism*, The Museum of Modern Art, New York, 1989.

Seckel, Hélène, *Les Demoiselles d'Avignon*, Musée Picasso, Paris, 1988.

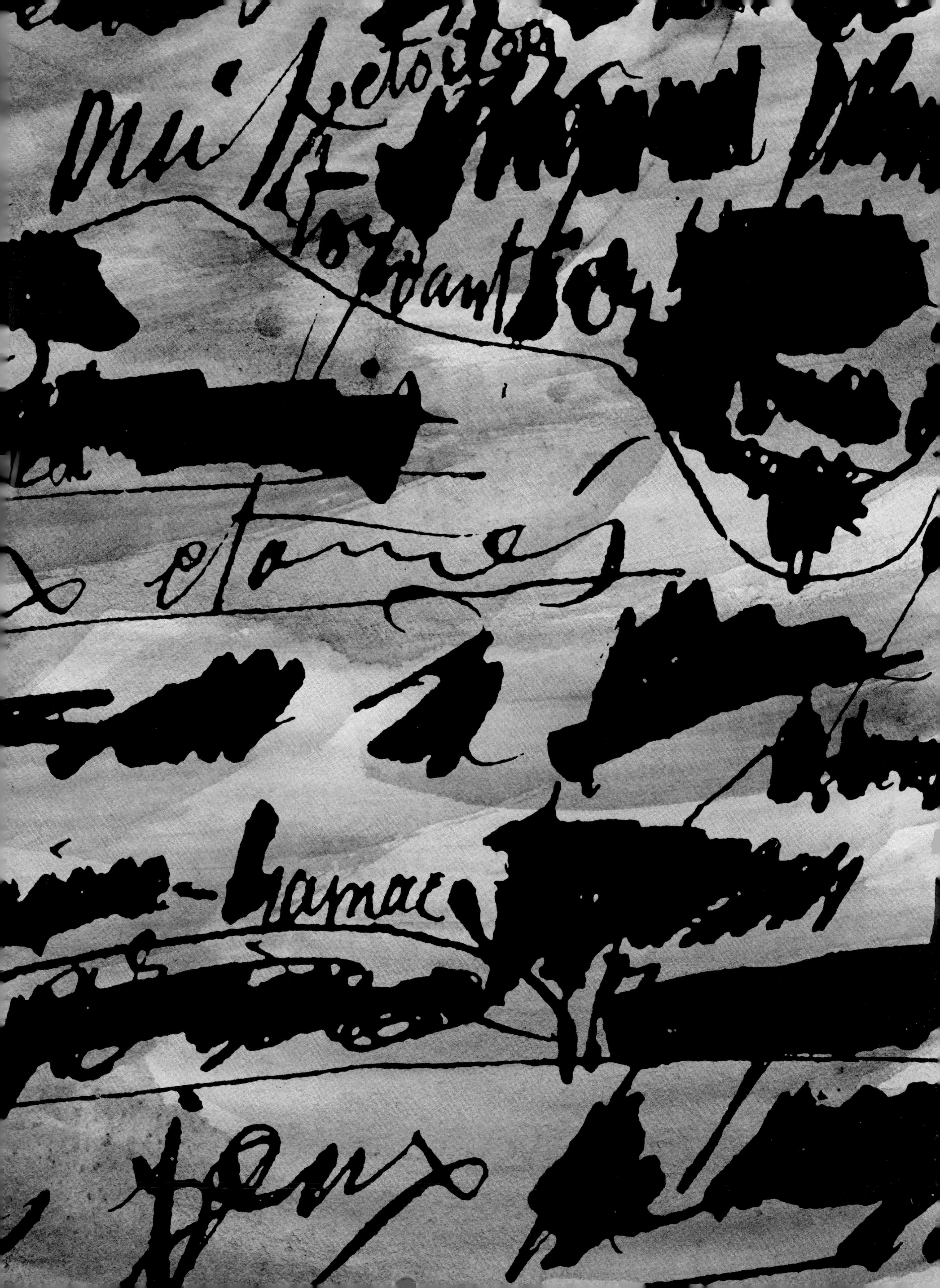
hamac